MW01289547

Breaking The Man Code:

"Unlocking the Key to His Heart"

By: Shawnda Patterson

TABLE OF CONTENTS

DEDICATION

This book is dedicated to my father, whose words I carry with me always. I know you are looking down from heaven and I hope you are proud of the woman I have become, for it was largely because of you. To my mother, the sweetest, kindest and most amazing person on this rock we call Earth. To my loving husband, you are the love of my life and my best friend. I am honored to be your wife. Thank you for encouraging me to write this book and, more importantly, to go after every one of my dreams. For that, I will be eternally grateful. To my three beautiful daughters, only God can love you girls more than your father and I do. Never forget Matthew 19:26, "...with God all things are possible."

"Love is only a word, until someone arrives to give it meaning. Don't give up. Remember, it is always the last key on the key ring that opens the door."

~ Paulo Coelho

INTRODUCTION

This book picks up where my last book, "The Dating Game: How to Find Yourself While Looking for Mr. Right" left off. My last book was all about your journey of self-discovery. We talked about confidence, knowing your worth, and establishing and maintaining your standards, among other things. This book is almost entirely about men! Can't live with them, can't live without them, so we might as well learn to understand them. I have poured my heart and soul into this book in hopes that you will find whatever it is you are looking for. Despite the heartaches and heartbreak, your search for love continues because you know when it is good, there is nothing like it! It is unequivocally the most incredible feeling in the world. For years, I have advised women regarding matters of the heart. I have done so because I believe that every woman deserves to be loved, cherished, appreciated and adored by a man who is worthy of her. Perhaps you may have seen some of my work online, so you have come to expect my no nonsense style. This book is no different. We cut right to the chase. In this book, you will discover answers to questions like, "Am I being played?" "How do I decode his mixed signals?" "Can men handle strong women?" "When is a man relationship ready?" and so much more. Want answers? Keep reading.

CHAPTER ONE

When NOT to Date Him

Before we talk about him, let's first talk about you. Be honest with yourself about why you want to be in a relationship. Never enter into a relationship for validation or to fill the void of loneliness. Both the need for validation and the fear of being alone demonstrate a lack of self-confidence and an unhealthy dependency on the approval of others. Embrace your uniqueness and learn to love your own company. After all, if you don't enjoy your own company, how or why would anyone else? Savor these single moments. You have the rest of your life to be someone's wife, but this moment is yours to do with what you will. Do not be in such a rush to be with someone that you don't appreciate the amazingness of this alone time. Finding companionship should be about you wanting to share your amazing life with someone with whom you can share true intimacy. Intimacy is not strictly a physical relationship, although that has its place as well. It is a deeper and more spiritual connection, better said, "In to me see." True intimacy is allowing yourself to be completely and utterly vulnerable with someone without the fear of having that vulnerability taken advantage of. It is not just allowing someone to see the "you" that you portray to the world, but the real you minus any of the filters we often use. That includes your silly side, sexy side, sensitive side and spiritual side. Before you question whether *he* is ready to date, you must first discover if you are aware of who you are, your gifts, your purpose, your strengths and your weaknesses.

Life happens in phases and seasons. Singleness is a season and seasons change. During this time of singleness, you should be on a journey of self-discovery and personal growth. Take an introspective look at yourself and make sure you like the reflection of the person you see staring back at you. What I am about to say may go against everything you have ever believed about being a single woman, but here goes...when you are a single woman, finding a man is not your sole mission in life. Boom! To some of you that is no great revelation, but to others it may go against everything you have ever been taught. Let me be clear. Being in a fulfilling, committed and monogamous relationship is important. In fact, the Bible says in Genesis 2:18, "It is not good for the man to be alone; I will make him a helper suitable for him" (NIV). However, life is about discovering your purpose and the reason for your existence. A mate can provide you with companionship and support while you are discovering, cultivating and walking in that purpose. But, being a wife is not the only reason you were created. Your mission is to become the absolute best version of yourself possible. As Gloria Steinem said, "Far too many people are looking for the right person, instead of trying to *be* the right person." Later in this book, we will discuss in depth how to become the ultimate woman, but before you seek certain things in a man, you must first seek to find them in yourself.

Not every man you date is meant to be your husband, soul mate or father of your unborn children. The approach you should take toward dating is to spend some time getting to know someone to see if there is a deeper connection. If there is, explore it and see where it takes you. If there is no connection, date another guy. I know this may sound like oversimplification, but we as women sometimes have to get over the urge to nurture and fix anything (or anyone) that is broken. We often focus on what a man could be as opposed to realizing who or what he actually is. In psychology, this is often referred to as the "halo effect." The halo effect is a cognitive bias in which an observer's overall impression of a person, company, brand, or product influences her feelings and thoughts about that entity's character or properties. I heard this saying once that goes, "Give a man ten women and he'll keep looking. Give a woman ten men and she'll choose." Sometimes without even fully realizing it, we begin to settle. Take this example for instance. We have all been there. You are shoe shopping and you spot the perfect pair of heels. You have been looking for these shoes everywhere for what seems like forever. You are a size seven and a half, but the only pair left is a size seven. So, you try them on and, unsurprisingly, they are tight. You know they're uncomfortable, you know they don't not feel right, you know they're painful, but you want them so badly you buy them anyway. You can't resist the urge to make them work. That does not work for shoes, and it definitely does not work for men and relationships. Never settle for a man just because you are afraid another one will not come along. It is okay to leave that pair of shoes on the shelf being fully confident you will find another pair you will love just as much, if not more. We often make our love decisions based on two emotions: fear and love. We sometimes base our decisions on the fear of never finding love. That fear sometimes causes us to enter into and maintain relationships we know we should not be in. We stay in these bad relationships because we don't want to be alone, but being alone is no worse than being with someone who makes you feel alone or like you are all alone in your relationship. A few months ago, I decided to reorganize my closet. I placed my items into four separate categories: keep, donate, sell and trash. I decided to sell anything new with tags and gently used to one of those popular cash for clothing stores. I strolled in there confidently with my two garbage bags filled with amazing pieces. The sales associate told me to come back in an hour while they assessed what my items were worth. I returned in an hour, secretly expecting to be blown away by the amount they were willing to offer me for my clothes. What an anticlimactic experience. The amount she offered me was downright insulting. In my utter shock I said, "Are you serious? Most of the items in these bags are brand new." She replied indifferently, "I know but..." and she gave me a "take it or leave it" look. I started gathering the bags. She said, "No no, we want to buy your things." Then I replied, "I know but not for that price." You can't be afraid to walk away when someone's best offer is not good enough. Resist the urge to settle while dating. As my mother always tells me, "What you compromise to get you must compromise to keep."

A man's approach to dating is quite different from a woman's approach. Men are always trying to qualify or disqualify you into two major categories. Although there are several subcategories such as friend zone and one night stand, most men classify women into two main categories. The first is the type of woman he can take home; the second is the type of woman he can take home to meet his mother. Which type of woman he is looking for at the moment depends on what stage he is in (in his life). This has nothing to do with how old he is; it has more to do with his level of relationship maturity. When a man meets you for the first time he is instantly trying to determine exactly what category you fall into. He makes a snapshot assessment of you based on a number of factors. However, his opinion of you is subject to change. You can easily shift from one category to another in an instant. He considers everything from the way you are dressed, the types of pictures you post on social media, if you allow him to be touchy feely with you early on, if you are being the aggressor, how open you are to his advances and more. If he has disqualified you in his mind as a potential mate, he may still pursue you because men are hunters by nature. Just because a man is pursuing you does not necessarily mean he wants to be in a relationship with you.

Only time and patience will reveal his true motives. Some men date women merely for sport. They want to see if their "game" is good, so they put it to the test. If their "game" is in fact good, they want to see exactly how many women it will work on. Much like an actual hunter mounts a deer's head above his fireplace as a trophy, some men add notches to their belts as a sign of their manhood and masculinity. This isn't a game solely played by boys; there are men well into their thirties, forties and fifties who are still playing these types of games. Never ever fall in love with a hunter because he cannot resist the urge to hunt. He will not be satisfied with anything (or anyone) he catches. Hunters enjoy the process, but not the reward. It's like a hunter who spends hours tracking down a deer, shoots it, but leaves it in the woods. It was never about the deer; it was all about the thrill of hunting big game. Do not allow your female ego to make you think it is possible for you to change this type of man. Truth is, men change when they are good and ready and not a moment before. You can't sex him enough, take care of him enough financially, or guilt trip him enough to make him commit to you.

I am almost ashamed to admit this, but I watch the television show "Cheaters" from time to time. My husband makes fun of me for doing so. He says it's the same thing every episode. I guess you can call it my guilty pleasure. I watched an episode once where there was a woman who found out her boyfriend had been cheating on her. She confronted him at a restaurant. He was caught red handed on a dinner date with another woman. The moment he saw the girlfriend running towards him outraged, he knew he was busted. He apologized profusely and told her he was thankful for everything she had done for him. She kept saying, "After all I've done for you." She literally ripped the shirt off his back. She even took a brief moment from this highly charged altercation to eat some French fries off his plate. While doing so she said, "I paid for all of this anyway." In a moment of clarity, she tearfully revealed to the host that she had given him a place to stay, food and clothing, and she put her dreams on hold to help him pay for his education. She was clearly upset and hurt that despite her best efforts to be supportive of her boyfriend in every way she knew how (mentally, physically, emotionally, sexually, and financially), it still wasn't enough to keep him faithful. As sad as that was to watch, I have seen similar situations in countless letters written to me, letters from women who gave their all in relationships that left them feeling empty and broken.

I want to talk about the best and the worst time to enter into a relationship with a man to help spare you from this type of heartache and pain. He must be ready or, no matter what you do, it will never be enough. I think the whole idea that men don't want to get married or don't want to be in a committed relationship is one of the biggest lies ever told. It's not a matter of *if* they want to be in a relationship; it is more so a question of ***when***. Marriage for both men and women is all about the timing. It is entirely possible to meet the right man at the wrong time. So, let's talk about some of the worst times to enter into a relationship with a man. Much like the story I just mentioned, dating a man while he is in some sort of transition in his life is definitely not the right time. Here are some examples of life transitions: he just had a baby (with another woman no less); his marital or relationship status is unresolved; he is newly separated, newly divorced, in the middle of a custody battle, or going through a divorce or a breakup; he is trying to establish himself financially; or he's searching for a career. A man in these types of situations can and mostly likely *will* be distracted. Entering into a serious relationship with any woman may be the furthest thing from his mind. A man who is recently separated, newly divorced or getting over a breakup most likely is not expecting the first woman he dates after his ex to be "the one." So, he may be especially cautious about moving too quickly into a new relationship or letting his guard down enough around you to allow you the opportunity to get to know him on a deeper level. Unfortunately, he could also be bitter and jaded towards all women. If the breakup or divorce was not his idea, he could still be holding out hope of reconciliation with his ex. Either way, there is far too much uncertainty and too many unresolved issues to deal with. Giving him time to heal will give him the closure he needs to be ready for a new relationship. The second worst time to get into a relationship with a man is when he is fully immersed in his bachelor lifestyle. I knew a man well into his sixties who had never been married. He entered into several relationships with one foot in and one foot out. There were countless women over the years who tried to make an honest man out of him, but he never allowed himself to get comfortable or too attached. I call this type of man the eternal bachelor. No matter how well you think things are going or how close you think you both are to an actual commitment, you find him saying things like, "We're just friends," "I'm not the relationship type," "We have a good thing going on here, so we shouldn't complicate things," and the ever popular, "You and I know what we have." He has a classic case of commitment phobia. You know the type - he's never met your family and friends, he only makes short term plans with you, you feel him pulling away every time things get a little serious, he gives you his undivided attention whenever you're together, but when you're not he's hard to find, and he occasionally disappears without explanation. He is the king of no strings attached dating. He will never allow you to get close enough to disrupt the life he has become so accustomed to. Women have been trying unsuccessfully for years to get him to settle down. He is not a bad guy; he just knows exactly what he wants and being in a committed relationship with one woman is not one of those things. This man is content in his singleness. If only we women could relish being single as much as he does. The third reason a man is not ready for a relationship is that he dreads the responsibility of it all. He could be overwhelmed by the thought of having to be responsible for someone else, not to mention he is not excited about handing over his player card. He is not interested in bringing his bachelor days to an end. He'd rather be hanging out with the guys or watching ESPN's Thirty for Thirty alone on his couch in his boxers than selecting wedding invitations and filling out the wedding registry at Williams Sonoma or Crate and Barrel. Simply put, he is not ready and readiness is key for a man. Men do not like to feel rushed or pushed into relationships. Have you ever known anyone who got married merely because the woman gave a man an ultimatum? It's quite sad actually. These types of relationships are often void of love and romance. He doesn't make a big deal about birthdays or Valentine's Days, and he often forgets anniversaries. Men who have been pressured into a stage of a relationship they were not ready for simply oblige your request but give nothing more. It is almost as if they resent you for taking away their choice. If a man tells you he is not ready for a relationship, that is exactly what he means. Lastly, and this one is probably the biggest hit to the female ego, he may simply not be into you. It is not that he doesn't want to get married, he just does not want to get married to you. Most of us have seen situations where a couple has been together for years and never gotten married; yet, months or a few short years after they break up, he marries someone else.

Now that we have established some of the worst times to expect a man to be willing to enter into a fulfilling relationship, let's talk about some of the best times. When a man is where he wants to be financially and career wise, he is very likely to be seeking companionship. He may consider it the missing piece to his life puzzle. By nature, men are providers and protectors, and once they feel they can adequately handle both of those tasks, they need someone to provide for and protect. They are ready for a wife and possibly children. He is most likely a homeowner with a car and a decent job. Although some men are guilty of the Peter Pan syndrome and they never want to grow up, at some point they do. They look in the mirror one day and realize there's gray in their beard or their hairline is slightly receding. They suddenly realize they are not twenty-one anymore. Now they are thirty, thirty-five or even forty, and they don't want to be alone the rest of their lives. These are the retired bachelors, the George Clooneys if you will. They are distinguished gentlemen who are very well established and have everything they want except the loves of their lives. They are best known for a string of pseudo relationships with random women. They are tired of playing the field. The reformed bachelor is ready for a meaningful relationship. He probably is not interested in having an intimate relationship with you right away. After all, he's already done that, remember? No strings attached and sex is no longer his primary concern. Nowadays, he is more interested in finding out if you would make a suitable wife and mother. He is straightforward and direct in his approach because he realizes he has no time to waste.

Remember, for men, it's always about timing. Men are most likely to commit when they are financially secure, ready for children and done playing the field. We will talk later in this book about relationship readiness. It is important to note that the love of a good woman can *make* a man ready. Marriage and children may have been the furthest thing from his mind until he met you. As the old saying goes, "The heart wants what the heart wants." Some men meet the right woman and they're ready to give up their bachelor lifestyle instantly. Some men simply decide, "It's time." In the show, "Sex in the City," Miranda, one of the main characters says, "Men are like cabs. When they're available, their light goes on. They wake up one day and they decide they're ready to settle down, have babies, whatever... and they turn their light on. The next woman they pick up, boom, that's the one they'll marry." For women, it's all about how we feel because we are emotional creatures; but, for men, it's always about timing.

So, you've met a new guy and you're wondering if this is the right time for him. Is his "available light" on? We've all encountered men who say all the right things. They say they're ready to get married and have children. Although he has not clearly stated he wants to do those things with you, you can't help but have those thoughts in your mind. Gotcha! For some men, that's a part of their game plan. Men know women have certain buzzwords or triggers that get our emotions running high, make our heart skip a beat and make our eyes light up. So, these buzzwords and triggers are strategically placed in their conversations with you to see how you react. Make no mistake, a man who attempts to sweep you off your feet or shamelessly shower you with love and attention is not necessarily a bad guy with ulterior motives. However, you would be wise to meet such grand gestures with a certain degree of skepticism.

Understandably, this has already become one of your defense mechanisms. Your hard outer shell is how you protect yourself from getting hurt. I get it. Not every man needs or deserves access to the innermost parts of you. But, if your outer shell is *too* impenetrable, you will run the risk of blocking out real love. This book was not written to make you afraid of love or afraid of being vulnerable. This book is to help you to determine when to be vulnerable and who it's safe to be vulnerable with. By now, you're probably asking yourself, "How exactly do I do that?" This is when it will be necessary to tap into your intuition or the spirit of discernment. We all have a God given ability to understand the spirit (or motives) behind something. Truthfully, some of us do not pray, use discernment or follow our intuition because we don't want to know. But, there are always warning signs and red flags. Sometimes we chose to ignore them until they refuse to be ignored. Before you allow yourself to get emotionally attached to someone, make sure you have prayed and asked God first. John 10:27 says, "My sheep listen to my voice" (NIV). The better your relationship with God, the easier it will be to hear from Him regarding the intentions of your new love interest. This is the best way to avoid heartbreak. And, for those of you who aren't religious, use your intuition as your guide.

I believe one reason people don't realize they are being played is because the player has put in the time and effort to make them feel comfortable. A true player is a chameleon. He will adapt, adjust and morph himself into whatever it is you want or need him to be. This is why it is so important that you never over share. Be careful about how much you divulge to a potential suitor. For example, it is your first date and you're nervous, so you're doing most of the talking. You notice he's just sitting back and listening attentively. If he is in fact a player, he will become the man you say you want. You told him on your first few dates that your ex never complimented your appearance and he never made you feel beautiful. The player will go out of his way to prove to you that he is different. He will constantly tell you how attractive he finds you. He'll let you know you look amazing in that dress. Not to be confused with a good guy, it's all about the intentions behind the words. Never give a man the blueprint for your heart. Of course, you want to allow him the opportunity to get to know you but you can do so without exposing your insecurities, ones that could be exploited by the wrong man. Players are always looking for a weakness to exploit. They want the most physical intimacy for the least amount of effort. Over sharing with a man is the surest way to end up being manipulated. So, you don't want to tell him you are insecure about your weight, your looks, your past etc. Allow him the opportunity to reveal himself and his true intentions. You do that by listening to him and asking the right questions. Questions like, "What would you consider to be the happiest moment of your life?" "Have you ever been in love?" "How long was your longest relationship, and when did it end?" "Do you believe men and women can just be friends?" "Do you believe in love at first sight?" "Are you religious?" "If your love life was a movie title, what would it be called?" You would be amazed at how much the right questions will reveal about a man. Ask the standard first date/interview sounding questions and get the standard first date answers. I would much rather say he lied to me than to say I never asked. Be upfront and direct with him early about your intentions and see how he reacts. For example, "I am not interested in a casual- no- strings- attached- sexual- relationship at this stage of my life. I am ready for something real." Study his reaction to that statement. Allow him to initiate further contact after that. If he never asks you out again, it is pretty clear that you both did not want the same things. Never underestimate the spirit of discernment. As a believer, I must recommend praying about any potential suitors. Ask God to reveal their intentions to you. Ask him to show you who they really are, not the image they are trying to portray. 1 Samuel 16:7 says, "...People look at the outward appearance, but the Lord looks at the heart" (NIV). Ask God to search his heart for anything that is not pure and genuine. Do not allow a man to waste the prime of your life while making you feel like you are not relationship material. When a man truly believes you are "the one," or at least have the potential to be, he is not going to let you just walk out of his life that easily. Most likely, he has dated so many women trying to find you that he is not willing to let you go and start all over again. "He who findeth a wife findeth a good thing," remember?

A lot of women believe in the fairytale. We would love to be caught up in a whirlwind romance and swept off our feet by our very own Prince Charming. I want to remind you to stay grounded. Make sure a man's words match his actions. Get what you want out of a relationship. If you know you want to be in a committed relationship with a man but he's offering you everything but that, you have to be strong enough to walk away. You could be in a relationship with a man who is being completely honest with you about his past hurt and pain. Allow him time to heal. Waiting around for the day he realizes you are worth the risk is wasting valuable time. Time you could be spending with a man who is relationship ready. If you have been played before, don't feel too badly because most of us have been. We were too naive, too trusting or too eager to believe some guy was too good to be true. We let our guard down once and we paid dearly for it. The good news is, "That which does not kill me can only make me stronger." You have learned from these mistakes. My hope is that this chapter has helped you to identify when a man is setting the foundation, being a pseudo boyfriend or becoming a chameleon.

CHAPTER TWO

How to Know if You are Being

Played

There is a fundamental difference in the socialization process of little boys vs. little girls. Little girls are raised with the idea of finding a well-established young man to marry and have children with. However, on the opposite end of the spectrum, little boys are encouraged to date more than one girl. In fact, older brother, uncles or maybe even his father beam with pride when he announces he has a few love interests. He is celebrated for the same behavior they would admonish if it were done by a girl. So, she grows up wanting to be with one man and he grows up wanting to be with every woman. This is the man your parents warned you about saying, "He is only after one thing." By now, we have met one, two or twenty men like this. His approach is so obvious and blatant he is easy to identify. He is a smooth talker and he is fearless. For him, it is all a numbers game. He's not genuine when he approaches women, but he knows the more women he approaches the more likely his chances are someone will say yes. He has no problem walking up to a group of women and striking up a conversation because he feels he has nothing to lose. If he's shot down he will simply regroup and find another woman to approach. A man who is too confident in his approach is comfortable because he does it all the time. Never mistake his ability to confidently approach you for a genuine desire to get to know you. When it comes to men assume nothing. Allow him to prove everything.

Are you being played? Have you been played? Truthfully, you may not even be sure. He was a great guy; things just didn't work out. Are you sure about that? Before you answer let's start by defining what a player really is. A player is a man whose sole intentions are to have sex with you with little or no commitment. Of course he would like to do this with little to no complications. The last thing he wants is to have you slashing his tires, keying his car or throwing his clothes out the window of your fourth floor apartment. He approaches dating like a robbery. He cases the joint (i.e. watches you to determine which technique will yield his desired results the fastest). When the time is right, he does the old smash and grab. He's in and out of your life so quickly you barely know what hit you.

Most players begin with their exit strategy. He may tell you a sob story about a recent painful break up or reveal how badly his ex-girlfriend broke his heart. If he is really good, he may be able to muster up some fake emotions and mention that he may never find the strength to love again. Yes, he lays it on thick. This does two things: it portrays him as this vulnerable and sensitive guy but, more importantly, it lets him off the hook in the future when you want any type of commitment from him. He wants to be able to say, "I told you from the beginning I was not ready for a relationship." Next, he *appears* to fall head over heels for you. By now, he has begun to give you his undivided attention. If he is not calling you he is texting you. Sometimes he is texting to tell you he is about to call you. There is the "good morning text, " the "how is your day going?" text, the "let's meet for lunch text," and the "call me when you are on your way home" text. This is his attempt to get you emotionally addicted to him. He is a gentleman at first, but it does not take long before the conversation escalates to being a bit more flirtatious and suggestive in nature. "What are you wearing?" "I hate sleeping alone. Don't you?" After all, that is the point of this secret agenda. On the surface, it seems like he cannot get enough of you. He is putting cheese in the trap girlfriend! This is commonly referred to as "love bombing." Beware of his attempts to influence you by lavish demonstrations of attention and affection. Finally, you have met your Mister Right, or so you think. He is showering you with all the attention and affection you have always dreamed of. It all feels like it's too good to be true. You do not want to get your hopes up, but in the back of your mind you start asking yourself could he be "the one?"

I know it is flattering especially if you are not used to getting this much attention, but this is all part of his plan. Although he has never formally requested to be your boyfriend you notice he behaves as if he is. His intentions are to get you used to having him around so you begin to expect him to be there. The more he continues this behavior the more you let your guard down and get more comfortable around him. You begin to expect things from him. You wait for those morning texts and those impromptu lunch dates and when you do not get them, you start to miss him. You start to feel like this is what life would be like if you were actually his girlfriend. So, you behave as if you are his girlfriend. In your mind, you have everything but the title right? That is when he knows he has you right where he wants you. The goal of a player is to get sex without commitment with a built in exit. That is exactly what I believed happened to the writer of this letter:

"When I first met this man we can call him Joe the first thing that attracted me to him, was that he genuinely cared about me and my well being. He is older than me by about 14 years, I am in my mid twenties. In the beginning everything was going great , we were going out on dates yaddahyaddahyaddah. Months go by and he still hasn't mentioned me becoming his girlfriend. He is always not open and doesn't give direct answers when I ask questions. So I start to wonder why....by this time I was caught up in feelings already as we would talk everyday throughout the whole day and always spent our time together. We also were intimate. We met in April '13 and by November '13 nothing had come up. I learn THEN in November that he had gotten out of a 4 year relationship 2 weeks prior to meeting me. He swears he told me when we first met that he didn't want a relationship and he had just gotten out of one but I know this not to be true because I wouldn't have stuck around in the beginning. Next March '14 I bring up being his GF and he basically says he's not ready and it's my choice to stick around and wait for him to "fix" himself. Unfortunately I was in love. So I stayed. June I bring up the fact that we should be saying I love you, because I had been feeling that way for so long. He basically tells me "he doesn't feel that way, why would I say that when in March he already told me how he felt". He says that he sees himself taking care of me mentally physically and spiritually. You would think this would make me leave...it didn't. It didn't make sense. I believe actions speak louder than words, and his actions always showed me he loved me. Which is why I have waited. He would surprise me and bring me roses at work, he would give me advice he acted like a boyfriend in every way possible, except calling me his girl, which I now believe to be the worst insult. My family and friends didn't understand it either. I was fed up. November '14. He had two weeks left and I was going to end it. (after watching your videos it gave me courage HA) Right at that time he finally says I love you and that we are a couple, but he won't use the word

GF. January '15 he meets my dad, mom, and brother for the first time. And NONE of them trust him, they all feel he is wrong for me. They say he is nice but he seems to be hiding something. They felt like he was glassy and the list goes on. His not being straight forward, not willing to say GF has led me to have feeling of distrust over our time together...he travels all the time for work. I feel like I already know the answer but I need you to help me see the truth. Hearing it from family is not quite the same."

As the late Maya Angelou once said, "We are as blind as we want to be." We often ignore the red flags and warning signs because we want to believe so desperately our search for "the one" is over. Do not get so caught up in your emotions that you are not noticing behavioral inconsistencies. For example, if he tells you he really cares deeply for you and he is not strictly pursuing you for sex, yet he cannot keep his hands off you, that is a blatant inconsistency and his actions have overridden his words. If you are not sure, test him to make sure what he says and what he means are one in the same. Throw him completely off guard by asking things like, "Do you say these things to all the girls?"And study his reaction. Years ago, I was being pursued by a young man. He was handsome and very romantic. In fact, he once gave me a beautiful poem. He said I was his muse for the piece. Needless to say, I was genuinely flattered. Well, some time had passed and he said he had another poem for me. Again, I was flattered and I could not wait to read it. After the first few words I noticed that it sounded eerily familiar. It was the exact same poem he had already given me before. He awaited my reaction as I read it, completely oblivious of his mistake. *So, he really does say this to all the girls,* I thought to myself. Once he was exposed as dishonest, I lost all interest in him. He was clearly a player and players know women are very emotional beings so they do or say certain things in hopes of eliciting an emotional response. They know if they can make their way into your heart you will be putty in their hands. Remember, men are hunters. It is amazing the lengths they would go to just to get what they want, spending money on you, getting to know your child, meeting your parents. Make no mistake; not every man is trying to take advantage of you. This story is a cautionary tale. I want you to be aware that there are some men with bad intentions, so be careful. This is why I do not believe in the 90 day rule. Yes, a good guy has no problems waiting 90 days, but so does a bad guy. The deadline is arbitrary. It is not about waiting a specific amount of days; it is about waiting to get to know someone. The longer you delay sex, the clearer a man's true intentions are to identify. Yes, he wants to sleep with you. He would never have asked you out if he did not. The real question you should be trying to answer is, "Is that all he wants?" Is this love or lust for him? Does he want to get to know you on a deeper level? Is he asking you the types of questions that lead you to believe he has a genuine interest in getting to know you? Go beyond surface level questions like, "How was your day?" Is he asking you, "Have you ever been in love?" "How do you imagine your life to be in 5 years?" Or does his conversation always end up becoming sexual in nature? Does he comment constantly about how attracted he is to you or how amazing your body looks? If you are receptive to this type of flirting he will break the "touch barrier." Basically, he will find any and every reason to touch you. The hugs become longer and the kisses become deeper. He may place his hand at the small of your back as you're walking together. Side note: avoid men who pressure you to have sex with them on the first date. His intentions couldn't be any clearer. At this point, he thinks he has you right where he wants you. Don't fall for it! This has all been a set up to get you to this point. He will push to be intimate with you and some women give in because this is their boyfriend right? Wrong! Once you've been intimate with him you'll begin to see him change. He is not as attentive and caring as he once was. You may notice that nowadays he takes forever to answer your calls or text messages. He can't seem to find time to get together with you when he used to drop everything to see you. So, while you are sitting in your living room leaving your third angry message in a row saying, "I have been trying to talk to you all day! Where are you?" it dawns on you...you have been played. "But he seemed like such a nice guy." We have all been there.

I saw a meme once that read, "Never use my love against me as a weapon." That is exactly what happens in these scenarios. A player does his homework. He has studied you thoroughly. He will adapt, adjust and morph himself into whatever it is you want or need him to be. If all you ever wanted was a good quiet guy, he will become that. If you just wanted a man to take you out on dates and tell you you're beautiful, he will be that too.

There are ways to avoid being played. Be leery of men who are all about the low cost romance. He wants to take you to the park, out for coffee or out for ice cream. Allow me to be frank here - dating is expensive! Have you seen how much movie theaters charge for popcorn and candy these days? My goodness! Players will be reluctant to spend money on you. They'll ask you to come to their place so they can cook for you or tell you they've already eaten so ice cream sounds great. If you notice he clearly has money to spend but he spends little to no money on you, he could possibly be a player. He never calls you in advance. For example, he calls you on Friday morning asking if you'd be interested in going out that night. You notice he never has planned dates. Everything always feels last minute and spontaneous. If it feels like you were just an afterthought it may be because you are. Some men go through their list of girls, calling every one of them until they find one willing to allow them to come over to "chill" or "hang out" late at night. You may very well have been one of many girls he called that night. Don't be afraid to say, "That is a little too short notice for me," "Sorry, I'm just about to turn in for the night," or "Aww, that sounds great, but I have already made plans." You can also say something like, "You know I'm a girly girl. I have to do my hair, makeup, find me an outfit etc. I need at least a day in advance." He would prefer to text you rather than call you. He often disappears for days then reemerges as if nothing has happened. He was most likely entertaining someone else or a few someone else's. You don't have to answer every last one of his phone calls. I am not suggesting you play games and ignore his calls intentionally, but if he is in no rush to respond to you, don't be in a rush to respond to him. There is nothing like giving a man a taste of his own medicine. Always present yourself as a challenge. You may also notice his phone is always ringing or buzzing when he's with you, yet he always seems to miss your calls. Players are forgetful. It's not easy keeping all their lies straight. A man shouldn't have to keep his story straight if what he is telling you is true. Be especially careful around men who constantly have inconsistencies in their story. One minute he's saying he was dumped by his ex because he was too close to his family, then he's telling you he broke up with her because she cheated. Avoid overinvesting in uninterested men. Keep things light and casual until there is a formal level of commitment. For example, letting a man know that hugs and a small peck on the cheek are reserved for men you are not seriously dating. Do not allow him to get too touchy feely with you, kiss you or think he even has a chance at staying the night. Another tip is to avoid being his beck and call girl. Never drop any pre-made plans to spend time with him. Let him know your time is valuable as well and you will not have it monopolized by a man who you are not in a serious relationship with. Date other people. Do not give the gift of exclusivity to man that A. Has not asked for it or B. Hasn't earned it. Get rid of the notion that women who date more than one man at a time are in some way less classy. I said date, not sleep with. Make sure he knows he's not the only one keeping his options open. Be open and honest with him about the fact that you are looking for something serious (if you are) and you will not entertain relationships that are strictly physical. And lastly, do not just play hard to get, *be* hard to get. Allow him to chase you. A player needs to know you are holding back and you are strong in your convictions. I will be honest with you. He may not hang around, but that is a good thing. He will either rise to the level of your standards or he will quickly get bored with you and move on to his next target. Either way, your dignity is intact and you have lost nothing because you never fully gave him everything to start with. Preserve some things for your husband. Engaging in casual sex is like giving every child that competes in a sporting event or competition a trophy. If everyone gets the same reward no matter how well or how poorly they played the game, the trophy is not valued to the player.

Unfortunately, life is not a fairytale. When it comes to playing the game of love you have to use your head *and* your heart. The point of this chapter was not to make you scared to date or trust men but to avoid warning signs right from the beginning. Be careful not to overinvest, get too physical, or be his beck and call girl. A player can be very patient. Much like a hunter, some men have no problems investing the time necessary to get you in their bed. They do not mind being in the friend zone and they will wait there patiently until the right opportunity presents itself. Players are always trying to create the perfect setting. He would love to get you over to his place with dim lights and romantic music. Do not become seduced by the mood, the ambience and him saying all the right things. If he has already told you from the beginning he is not ready for a relationship, believe him. This is all one big elaborate ruse to seduce you. Don't misunderstand my point. No man earns your vagina like some huge stuffed animal that is won at your local county fair. No matter how mind blowing or Earth shattering the sex, you will not keep a man or make him change his mind about being in a relationship if he is not ready. The best way to avoid being played is not to appear desperate. Here are three actions and behaviors you may want to avoid: 1. Avoid one sided communication. It should not be solely your responsibility to initiate conversation via phone or text. Make sure he is also reaching out to you. Do not call him repeatedly. Call and leave a message and allow him to return your call. You're a busy woman with options too, remember? 2. Conduct yourself as a quality woman at all times. Be mindful of the images you post on social media and the conversations you entertain. There's nothing wrong with being a little flirty. In fact, I encourage flirting. That keeps you out of the friend zone in his mind. Over-sexualizing the conversation can make you appear desperate and confuse him about what kind of woman you really are. 3. Maintain your standards. For example, if you have made it clear to him you do not kiss on the first date yet you allow him to kiss you, he may feel like your standards are just talk. He may question and or test how committed you are to all of your standards. If you do not take your standards seriously, neither will he. Never settle for friends with benefits either. Be honest enough with yourself to admit you want and deserve more than this. You want a real relationship, but you settle for this because it is all he is offering. So, out of sheer desperation you accept his offer and delude yourself into believing you are both getting exactly what you want from this arrangement. Well, you are half right. A man does not put you in this position; this is a position you have put yourself in. If you have found yourself here it is either because there is something about you or your personality he does not find appealing, or he realizes he does not have to offer you more because you have not made it a non negotiable term or condition. A man being intimate with you with no real feelings, emotions or commitment is not your friend and he does not genuinely care for you or your well being. He just says you're friends to make you feel a bit less cheap. A player will do or say whatever it takes to get exactly what he wants from you. He is merely taking advantage of a situation and exploiting what he has identified correctly as a lack of self-esteem. Do not delude yourself. Your willingness to accept this arrangement speaks louder than words. Despite how much you proclaim this is what you want, you would not be reading this book if you did not want more. You may lie to me, but you cannot lie to yourself. The millisecond you stop allowing him access to your body he will simply move on to someone else. If he cared so much for you, why doesn't he mind if you see other people? He may not want you to be intimate with other men, but that is not because he cares; he does not want you to establish the same friends with benefits arrangement with someone else. He is merely looking out for his own interests. Additionally, a man who is comfortable with such an arrangement is most likely being intimate with other women or wants the freedom to do so. Men like this treat women like rental cars. When you are in a rental car you are not nearly as careful or as meticulous with its care as you are with your own car. Why? Because there is no personal investment. You are merely using it and when you're done with it, you return it with little regard for its condition. Do not let a man treat you like a rental car. Do not allow him to use you up and then leave you with absolutely nothing to give your future husband. You are worth so much more than a no strings attached commitment free "situationship." You are a Proverbs 31:10 woman, and that verse reads, "Who can find a virtuous woman? For her price is far above rubies" (NIV). Always remember a man does not define your worth, you do. If you constantly find yourself in this type of situation, you have to realize the common denominator is you. You have to take full responsibility for your part in this. What is it about you that attracts this type of man? A mistake made repeatedly, whether consciously or unconsciously, is a choice. This often stems from a lack of self-esteem and a thought or feeling that this is all you deserve or the best that you can do. We teach people how to treat us by the way we treat ourselves. We reinforce our standards by sticking to them no matter the consequences. Your standards cannot be contingent upon your feelings.

CHAPTER THREE

Men and Commitment Phobia

Why can't real life be more like those romantic movies we have watched for years? Why can't men say things like, "I came here tonight because when you realize you want to spend the rest of your life with somebody, you want the rest of your life to start as soon as possible," just like Harry did in "When Harry Met Sally?" We all love a storybook ending, but not every man is going to be your Prince Charming. In fact, you need to be prepared to meet a few frogs along the way.

So, you have been seeing this amazing guy for a while now but for some reason things have sort of stalled. Could he be a serial casual dater? You know that type. He says his longest relationship has only been 3-4 months. And because he is so amazing you wonder why some lucky woman hasn't snatched him up yet. Are you sure he wants to be? He could have a common case of commitment phobia. Commitment phobia is defined as fear of lost options or fear of making poor decisions. Truthfully, there are several reasons this "catch" hasn't been caught. In this chapter, I'll give you several of the most common reasons he has not committed and may not want to.

1. He has baggage. He could still be recovering from a bad breakup with an ex girlfriend, or he just went through a painful divorce. For this reason, he has become very guarded and he is unwilling to allow anyone to get too close to him. This type of man is a hard nut to crack. The relationships in his past could have also left him very jaded. He may be very skeptical about the whole idea of love. After all, he was vulnerable with a woman once and she broke his heart. Who's to say you won't do the same? You both would be assuming an enormous risk

should you decide to pursue a relationship. He may be there physically, but emotionally he's unavailable.

2. He may be using you as a place holder. He's in no rush to be in a committed relationship, but he knows if he is honest with you about that you'll leave. He stays because he's comfortable around you and you get along fine (that is, when you're not asking him to define your relationship). He may be stingy with affection unless he thinks it may lead to sex. Secretly, he already knows you're not the one for him. He will waste as much of your life as you're willing to let him. He promises you if you are patient with him, one day (one day rarely comes) you will be rewarded for your loyalty and patience by getting to be his girlfriend or wife. This is the type of man who could be with a woman for several years without marrying her, breaks up with her and marries another woman in less than a year. This type of man is the worst. If you are not careful, he can rob you of your youth and vitality. Beware of a man who hasn't introduced you to anyone significant in his life, goes completely

MIA around the holidays, never initiates conversations, refuses to define your relationship and leaves you confused about exactly where you stand.

3. He may feel like being in a committed relationship is not a priority for him right now. We all have what I like to call a "life pie." We allocate certain slices of our life pie to the things that are most important to us such as family, friends, career, finances and love life. At this point in his life, he may be focused on finishing school, getting a management position at his job or buying his first home. Those things are more of a priority to him right now; therefore, they get a larger slice of his life pie. Pursuing and maintaining a committed relationship (even with someone as incredibly amazing as he thinks you are) may be something he is interested in, but he doesn't make it a higher priority than other areas of his life.

4. He may not feel the same way about you as you feel about him. He thinks you're attractive, funny, smart and fun to be

around but, for some reason, there's no spark. He may think you lack that certain "it" factor he's looking for. This in no way is a reflection on who you are and what you have to offer. It simply means the two of you are on different pages and may want something different from a life partner, nothing more.

5. He's not interested in giving up his current lifestyle. He may be ready for the white picket fence, the mortgage payments, the kids, etc., but he never wants to fall victim to what he believes to be the bait and switch. His biggest fear is that the confident, attractive, well-maintained sexy woman he marries will completely change and let herself go the moment the "I do's" are exchanged. He fears the carefree woman he fell in love with who seemed to enjoy cooking, cleaning and never putting up a fuss when he wanted to hang out with his friends will turn into a bathrobe wearing needy nag who guilt trips him about leaving her alone to be with his friends. He ultimately fears the death of his individuality and his freedom. Don't get me wrong – he loves spending time with you, but he also loves

spending time away from you and enjoying his "me time." He may love you or care deeply for you, but not enough to sacrifice his beloved sense of independence. Getting a man like this to commit may be difficult, but not impossible. I strongly advise against doing anything you cannot or will not maintain. The key is consistency. Throughout the course of your relationship, continue to do the things you did to get him in order to keep him. I recommend doing this for any and every relationship, but especially for relationships like this one.

6. He may not be done sowing his wild oats. Men love the thrill of the chase and he may still be in full-blown hunter mode. He may want a few more notches under his belt before he commits to you or anyone else. For him this could be a matter of right girl, wrong time. Men want different things at different times in their lives. At one point in his life, he may just be interested in a woman he can take home, and at another point in his life he may only be interested in women he can take home to mama. It's really all about what stage he's in in his life

and his level of maturity. If he tells you he is not ready for a serious relationship, it could be for any number of reasons. Here are a few: he actually has a girlfriend, he's not over his ex, he does not think you require one, he's not where he wants to be financially, he's not sure about his living arrangements, he's scared to trust his instincts again because he feels like they failed him in the past and he is not ready to be a one woman man.

7. He may not be willing to commit because you behave as if he owes it to you. You have made a habit of doing things for him he never requested. You've given him money, helped him with school, paid bills etc., and you think these good deeds have earned you the right to something. There is a sense of entitlement there he does not like. If you say things like, "After everything I've done for you…" No one likes doing things out of a sense of obligation. If you decide to go above and beyond for the man in your life, do it out of the kindness of your heart. Do not compile a list of good deeds to be thrown in his face or to

be used as leverage to get what you want from him. This almost always backfires.

8. He feels like you are pressuring him to commit. Committing to you is a step a man must make on his own. If not, he could begin to feel anger and resentment towards you for taking away his power of choice. Regardless of how much he loves or cares for you, being forced to move at your pace and not his is a major turn off. This shift or reversal in roles is not appealing to men because it goes against their very nature to be the pursuer and not the pursued. Insisting that he take this relationship to the next level only makes you look desperate. Desperation is the most unattractive characteristic a woman can possess. Men love confident women, remember? He likes the way things are and does not feel a need to change anything. This happens when a woman gives a man all the benefits of being in a committed relationship without actually being in one. She may be sleeping with him, dating him exclusively (whether he asked her to or not), living with him,

having children with him, cooking and cleaning for him etc. A man in a relationship with a woman willing to give him all of this does not have a good enough reason to change anything. There's a lot of talk about the male ego, but the female ego is pretty large as well. Hear me clearly – you will not sex a commitment out of a man. He may stay around a little longer so he can continue to enjoy this commitment free sex, but all you'll ever be to him is great sex. Men are fully capable of detaching themselves completely from sex, so being intimate with him does not increase your chances for building a genuine connection with him. However, a man who delays intimacy could be a keeper. I once dated a man who told me, "One day when you are my wife, we are going to have plenty of sex, but for right now I am fine with the way things are." Not all men are consumed with the thought of sex. Yes, at some point he would like to be intimate with you, but for now he may more concerned with finding out if you could qualify as a potential mate. Attempting to use sex as a weapon is an exercise in futility. I know you want him to get a sneak peek into what life *could* be like should he make the ultimate commitment to you.

You know in your heart you are perfect for him and you want him to see that. But, as the old saying goes, "Why buy the cow when you can get the milk for free?" If you are willing to give a man everything now what incentive would he ever have to change? Let me give you an example. Being with you should be like gaining access to an exclusive club. Only the VIP (very important person) will ever see what is beyond the velvet ropes.

If you are in a relationship and you feel as if your love interest is beginning to pull away, meet him at his level of engagement and restrict his access pass. If a man is telling you he is not ready for a relationship, believe him. No one knows him better than he knows himself. He knows if he is not done playing the field, he would like to be further in his career, or he's not completely over his ex girlfriend. Do not attempt to change him or change his mind. At this point, your only option is to stop investing so much time and energy into this relationship. The last thing you want to do is be in a relationship all by yourself.

This is why dating multiple men until you are given a commitment and a reason to be exclusive is so important. You too have options. Never volunteer to be exclusive with a man who has not asked you to or if the commitment level from him does not warrant it. Exclusivity is earned. It does not come standard. It lets a man know he has to earn the right to be the only man spending time with you. And, in situations like this one, if he feels like he is not ready for something more serious you can just put him in the casual dating category. This is when you also pull away. Do not allow him to be overly affectionate with you, spend the night or make any demands of your time. Make it clear to him that there is a distinct difference in the way you interact with a man you are casually dating as opposed to a boyfriend or significant other. Do not give men that you casually date boyfriend privileges. Men have to see the benefit in being exclusive with you and offering you more of a commitment. Re-establishing boundaries and upholding your standards lets a man know you are a catch. The idea that you would risk losing him because he has not risen to your level or standard may be the incentive he needs to pursue you more relentlessly. By doing all of this you have made yourself even more of a challenge. You are not being too pushy by making it clear to a man what you want and what you will or will not tolerate. Men love it when a woman sets boundaries and actually sticks to them. If a man thinks adhering to your standards is just too much work, he is probably not the right guy for you.

CHAPTER FOUR

He Who Findeth a Wife

Most little girls grow up dreaming of marrying their Prince Charming someday. Then, you get older and older and you start to wonder if it is ever going to happen. Before we delve into this chapter this let me first say being single does not mean there is anything wrong with you. Never forget you are fearfully and wonderfully made. Your relationship status does not define who you are as an individual. Yes, you would love to find companionship in the arms of a man who loves and appreciates you, but your value as a woman isn't dependent upon it. With all that being said, you may be reading this book because you want to know why your Boaz hasn't found you.

The answer may surprise you. I received this letter from a woman some time ago. She may sound quite a bit like you. She writes:

"This is my issue, when people (usually married men, women, colleagues - in other words, not eligible bachelors) find out that I am single they find it difficult to believe and I have been told more than once that I must have a load of men flocking my way. Sadly I don't.

I come from a very conservative Ethiopian background so I have never put myself 'out there' so to speak. I suppose my question to you is how to be 'found' by a good man with a view of finding love and something permanent. What is a girl to do?!

For so long I have not had any of this in my mind, naturally knowing that if it happens that is wonderful, but getting on with my life is more important. I still do, but as a feeling, breathing, lady, a wonderful masculine addition to my feminine life would be welcome.

Could you give me some idea on how to go into the hide and seek world of dating with a view to finding as grounded and as complete as I am. Where does one go and what does one do?

I should mention that my life typically revolves around my work, friends and family. (Married or long term partnered). I'm 29 almost 30.

Thank you so much.

Much love"

What I found most interesting about this woman's letter was she wanted to know how to be found by a good man. Whether you are a believer or not, you've likely heard the Proverbs 18-22 scripture, "He who findeth a wife findeth a good thing" (NIV). Although I agree wholeheartedly with this verse, I believe we tend to take it too literally sometimes. Let's break it down a bit shall we? The word find is defined as to recognize or to discover to be present. Are you putting yourself in a position to be recognized or discovered?

I recently hosted a single's retreat called "High Heels High Standards." It was a two and a half day event held in two luxury mountain cabins in Ellijay, GA. Twenty-three ladies came from coast to coast to be a part of the event. On the first night, we had an amazing heartfelt and emotionally charged discussion. One of the most commonly used phrases I heard was they were "waiting for Boaz." Let's also define wait. Wait is defined as to stay where one is or delay action until a particular time or until something else happens. Is that what you're doing? If so, no wonder you hate being single. I am not trying to insult you; I am just trying to make a point. Boris Paternak said, "Man was born to live, not to prepare to live."Some women play such a passive role in dating. They do the same thing over and over expecting a different result. How do you expect to meet someone new if you never "put yourself out there" like the woman said in her letter? I'm not suggesting you go on an all out manhunt. Don't wait in the bushes outside the club wearing camouflage and face paint. I challenge you to do something different!

Live your life. No one who has not offered you a commitment should earn the right to exclusivity. Stop waiting around for some man to realize and appreciate your value. I see this far too often. Take this letter I received for example:

"My friend is in a relationship with a man who I think is stringing her along. They have been in a relationship for about 6 years now. They started dating when he first moved to the area. He told her up front he had a kid and all about that relationship with the "ex". About a year after he moved there the kid came first and then his "ex" moved. His ex and his kid live in the same house and he tells her that nothing is going on. He won't kick her out because he claims that she'll ask for back child support and that it will be upsetting for his son. My friend has not meet either the son or the "ex", she can't visit him he only comes to her. He has said that once the child graduates from high school they will finally get married, which is now 2 years away. I really have been trying to get her to live her life instead of putting her life on hold for him. She is so intent on being married. She doesn't even want to travel without being married. I have offered several times to do a girls trip and it was always no. I really want to provide her with some hard evidence, what should I do? What other advice can I give her? I don't want two years to pass and she gets heart broken at the end."

The saying, "love is blind" could not be more accurate. Let me be clear. You are not a Capulet and he is not a Montague. Situations like this one are not modern day Romeo and Juliet love stories. You should not have to overcome these types of obstacles to be with someone. If he actually did love the woman in this letter, as I'm sure he has said he does, he would not put her in this type of position. A man who is truly into you would not allow you to cheapen yourself by making you the other woman, or allow it to look that way. Even the Bible makes reference to this in 1 Thessalonians 5:22, "Abstain from all appearance of evil" (NIV). Even if the man in this letter had the best intentions, it definitely doesn't appear that way. This is not what waiting on Boaz means. God would never give you someone else's boyfriend, fiancé or husband. So, if the man you are "waiting" for is still resolving issues with someone else, allow him to do that and then return to you once it is done. I cannot stress enough the importance of asking the right questions. There is not much difference between a lie and a lie by omission. Even men too eager to marry you can be hiding skeletons in their closets. Take this letter for instance:

"Hi BG!I met my husband and we hit it off, we fell in love so quickly it shocked us both, we knew that we wanted to be together because we began planning our future right away. We got married 3 months after meeting and also we are expecting our first child together. When we met I asked him how many children did he have and he stated that he had a daughter who was very young (She was almost 2 years old). I accepted his child and I love her as my own. Weeks after getting married I was thrilled that my husband and I would be having our first child together. Everything seemed to be falling right into place. I had a great relationship with my mother in law & sister in law, and my family seemed to love him as well. 3 months into my pregnancy my husband informed me that he needed to speak with me about his past. Right before we met, he had ended a relationship with a young lady who was expecting a child and during a breakup the woman before her was pregnant as well (Yes you read that correctly) One young lady was 9 months pregnant, & the other one was 7 months pregnant and I was now 3 months pregnant. I cried until I couldn't cry anymore, I screamed and I said I wanted out! He begged me to stay because he loved me and he didn't want to lose me. As the months have passed I have truly tried...I've prayed and asked God to remove this anger from my heart. I still have a relationship with his daughter but I can't bring myself to have a relationship with these other two children. He has not seen the children personally... only on pictures and social media. One child is now 6 months and the other is 4 months old. Our son can be born any day now & I still have a hard time with this matter. Thankfully even though I have been through so much stress my son is doing well. My world has been flipped upside down, during the middle of all of the madness his (Mama's boy instinct began to surface as well). His mom meddles in our business and completely over steps her title as mother vs wife. Any matters inside of our home, he calls her to talk to her about it. She recently began posting pictures of the other children on her social media (to further embarrass me) The mother's send him pictures of the children and I assume he sends them to her. I was so embarrassed that I didn't tell anyone about these children but that all changed when she began posting pictures and of course the questions began from everyone! I can't even explain how embarrassed I am to be married to someone that I feel like I can't trust, I barely like being in his presence because he can't understand why this is so hard for me. I also think that his mom did that to hurt me because she doesn't talk to me and neither does his sister anymore since I've had such a hard time dealing with these additional two children. I love him, but am I wrong because I can't stomach the idea of having a relationship with those other kids that I knew nothing about? I feel so betrayed, lied to and misled. I don't feel like he's the same person that he portrayed himself to be. I am seriously thinking of divorcing him. Please advise. xoxo"

There is a saying that goes, "Follow your heart but take your brain with you." As we discussed earlier in this book, men have an uncanny ability to identify desperation in a woman. They can tell when your eyes light up at the slightest mention of marriage. So, they dangle a ring in front of you like a carrot to see exactly how anxious you are to take the bait. Not all men are afraid of marriage (as demonstrated in the letter above). Do not let your desire to be married cloud your judgment and allow you to make rash decisions that are not well thought out. As in this letter, some men rush the relationship because they are hiding something. It is important to take your time in getting to know someone new. Lies by omission are just as dangerous as any other. If you feel like you are being swept off your feet in a whirlwind courtship, you have the power to slow it down. Do not be afraid to tell him, "I really care about you, but things are going a little too fast." The Bible says in 1 Corinthians 13 4-7, "4 Love is patient, love is kind. It does not envy, it does not boast, it is not proud. 5 It does not dishonor others, it is not self-seeking, it is not easily angered, it keeps no record of wrongs. 6 Love does not delight in evil but rejoices with the truth. 7 It always protects, always trusts, always hopes, always perseveres." (NIV). Despite how charming and seemingly perfect he may be, consider all those things. Is he patient? Is he kind? Is he easily angered? If you are genuinely considering spending the rest of your life with a man, make sure you know him as thoroughly as possible. Be sure to get answers to these questions before you begin to become emotionally attached because once you have done so, you may begin to overlook things that may have initially been deal breakers for you. Here are several great "get to know him better" questions:

"Have you ever been in love?"

"Do you believe we only get one soul mate?"

"How long was your longest relationship?"

"When did your last relationship end?"

"What is your relationship like with your family?"

"What was your childhood like?"

"Do you have any children?"

"How old are your children?"

"How long were you in a relationship with your children's mother?"

"What's your relationship like with the child's mother now?"

"Have you ever been to jail?"

"Would you consider yourself a Christian or just spiritual?"

"Do you believe more in God or fate?"

"What is it you are really passionate about?"

"Do you live alone?"

"Are you dating anyone else at the moment?"

"Do you have very many female friends?

"Have you ever cheated on a girlfriend?"

"Where do you see yourself in 5 years?"

"What steps are you taking to get there?"

"Who are your biggest inspirations?"

"What would you say is your biggest regret?"

"What is the best piece of advice anyone has ever given you?"

"Do you have a bucket list?"

"Would you mind sharing with me about a few things on your list?" (Offer to share a few of yours as well if he's hesitant.)

"How do you typically handle arguments?"

"Do you believe everyone has a purpose? If so, do you know what yours is?"

"What do you like to do in your free time?"

"What would you consider the perfect date?"

"What would you consider to be your greatest accomplishment?"

"What is your favorite thing about women?"

Of course, not all of these questions are first date appropriate, so you have to use your own discretion. Some questions are better suited for the third or fourth date, while some questions are better suited for a few months into a relationship. For example, "Where do you see this relationship heading?" "What is it that you love about me?" "If you could change something about me what would it be?" and "Do I make you happy?" By asking such direct and straightforward questions, you can find out if he's a workaholic, a commitment phobe, has a quick temper, lacks ambition, involved with other women and so much more. You would be amazed how much asking the right questions can reveal about a man. Listen intently. Had the writer of this letter taken her time and asked these types of questions, perhaps she would not have been in such a predicament. Do not be afraid to ask your questions. If he genuinely wants to get to know you and for you to know him, he should have no problems answering. Men who are secretive have something to hide.

Do not be in a hurry to get married. A wedding is only one day, but marriage is a lifetime. Some say men only care about one thing. The same could be said for us women when it pertains to marriage. In your early twenties people ask, "What's the rush?" By your mid twenties they ask, "Are you seeing anyone special?" By the time you're thirty they're not saying anything... not to your face at least. By now, you have enough ugly bridesmaids dresses hanging in your closet to start your very own online tackybridesmaidsdress.com e-business. You are genuinely happy for your friends and family who are tying the knot, but you can't help but wonder when it will be your turn. Sadly, some women feel like a wedding is the only way to validate they are worthy and good enough. Truthfully, you are good enough whether you are someone's better half or not. For a lot of us women, that is the entire point of dating. And I know you may want to tell a man on the first date that marriage is your ultimate goal, but it comes across as a bit too forward. Overemphasizing marriage to a guy or mentioning it too early can be a major turn off for him because you come across as insecure and anxious when you over share. Even men who ultimately want the same thing can be immediately turned off by your over enthusiastic desire to get married. Men never want to feel like you just wanted to get married, but like you just wanted to get married to him. So, when you make him feel like you already have the venue, catering, and wedding dress picked out and all you need is a groom, he feels insignificant, like you would have married him or any man who showed interest in you. As girls, most of us dreamed of our wedding day, but that is not typically the case for men. They never want to feel like this was just a right guy right time situation for you. No one wants to feel like getting married to you was just something you have been dying to scratch off your "to do" list. The idea of when to discuss marriage is a fairly controversial topic. Some suggest the first date, while others recommend you stay off the topic for at least a year. As long as the topic of marriage is introduced to the conversation organically, I would say anytime is the right time. Never resort to guilt tripping or pressuring a man into marriage. It just makes you look desperate. A quality woman realizes the one for her will not have to be forced, but will voluntarily and genuinely embrace the opportunity to share his life with her. He will consider it an honor and a privilege and not a chore or a burden. He will not need convincing. In Genesis 2:23 when Adam first sees Eve he says, "At last...This one is bone from my bone, and flesh from my flesh! She will be called 'woman,' because she was taken from 'man'" (New Living Translation). A man should exclaim "At last!" when he is with you, figuratively, not literally. His words and actions should demonstrate a feeling of "at last." He should be that grateful to have finally found you. This type of man does not need to be presented with ultimatums because he believes he "findeth a good thing." Be direct and make your objective clear without being overly repetitive. This is not a question or a proposition, but a declarative statement. For example, "My ultimate goal for dating is to find the man I love and want to spend my life with, get married and eventually have children. I'm not saying that man is you because we just met and I'm still getting to know you. And I'm not saying next week because it takes time to get to know someone but, for me, that is the whole point of all of this." Whether they know it or not, they should be on a clock. There should be a predetermined time table for the amount of time you date someone before elevating that relationship to the next level. I do not recommend sharing this timetable with a man because he will feel pressured and men want to feel like a decision this major was derived on their own. Much like your standards, you establish your own timeline and exactly how strictly you enforce it. This keeps you from maintaining long term relationships that are not going anywhere. Walking away from a man you are still in love with because the relationship is not progressing is difficult but necessary. If he truly loves you, he will not let you walk away. I know this is easier said than done, but if you do leave, make the break as clean as possible. Let him know this is not an attempt to give him an ultimatum, guilt trip him or pressure him, but you are not willing to give up on something that means so much to you. He will most likely tell you being married is just a piece of paper, but so is money and he values that. Being married is the ultimate demonstration of commitment. Some men will have children with you, buy homes with you and so much more, yet they say they are afraid of getting married. Some men know from the very start they never intend on getting married, but they do not want to lose you so they neglect to tell you that and they offer you everything but. They get you comfortable. They live with you and have children with you and hope this is enough for you to give up on the idea of marriage. These are all distractions that are designed to buy him time. This is your classic stall tactic. This is why you never allow a man to get too comfortable. From the very beginning you made your intentions clear and throughout the relationship you reminded him that certain things were reserved for your husband, like having children, living together and being intimate (I wholeheartedly recommend waiting until marriage). Be clear with him in saying I am not content with just playing house. I deserve and require a real commitment and I refuse to settle for anything less. I said this earlier on in this book, but it bears repeating – get what you want! This is not about accepting whatever a man offers you, but making sure his offer is in line with your standards and your own expectations of the life you want to live.

It is perfectly normal to want to get married. In our minds, we have an idea of the life we would like to live with our significant other and life is perfect. We want to go on ski trips, take a cooking class, go wine tasting or visit a bed and breakfast in Savannah, Georgia. My question to you is, why are you waiting? This is not to say you should choose someone rather than being with the man God has chosen for you, but what are you waiting on to begin living this amazing life you've imagined for yourself? Why can't you and a few of your girlfriends take a weekend ski trip or a cooking class? So many women believe their life will not begin until they meet their Mr. Right. But your life has already begun and it can be as amazing and fulfilling as you make it. Men are attracted to confident women, women who are not afraid to get out there and do things on their own. Incorporate him into your life without fully abandoning it for him. Don't expect a man to save you from your boring life; allow him to join you in your already amazing one. I saw a meme once that read, "This princess doesn't need saving" and neither do you. Who is to say you won't meet an amazing single guy while you are on your girlfriends' getaway, taking a cooking class, or at a summer festival in the park? I am not suggesting you become someone you aren't just for the sake of meeting a man. Most men will see right through that approach anyway. If you are not into the nightlife, try going to a different coffee shop than the one you usually go to. Try visiting your best friend's church, go to a poetry reading, go to a new museum exhibit or read your book at Barnes and Noble every now and then instead of at home. If you want to be found, you will have to do something different and put yourself out there, but do it in a way that's natural to who you are. Being single isn't a curse. You have the freedom and the opportunity to do so many things you've always wanted to do. Take this time to discover yourself. That's why I titled my first book, "The Dating Game: How To Find Yourself While Looking For Mr. Right." Your Boaz will recognize or discover you while you are on your own personal journey of self discovery. You can have an amazing life. Don't wait to start living it!

CHAPTER FIVE

Mixed Signals

I once received a letter from a young woman explaining that she was having communication issues with a man. Truthfully, in her mind, he was her man but he gave her the old, "I told you I'm not ready for a relationship" speech I discussed in the previous chapter. She said she asked him why he never calls her and he said it was because he had a horrible phone battery and his phone kept dying. She then asked why he doesn't text her more often, and he replied he would much rather call her and talk to her on the phone than send text messages. When they did actually speak on the phone she said their conversations only lasted about one to two minutes. I was appalled! Not so much because he did not call her more often, but because she allowed him to get away with it. Is he really sending her mixed signals? No. It is painfully obvious how he feels about her. We have all heard the saying "A man will only do what you allow" and that is exactly what happened here. You may be asking yourself how is it that one allows this type of behavior? You allow this type of behavior by not addressing it and setting real consequences for it. If she would like better and more frequent conversations with this man she should say something like, "I think you are a great guy. I understand you may not be ready for a relationship right now and that is okay, for now. But, if you are serious about getting to know me and possibly taking this relationship to the next level, I would like to speak with you more often. I am not a one to two minute conversation kind of girl." This confirms you are interested in him, but it also sends a clear message that you know what you deserve and you will not settle for anything less. As I said before, if a man is genuinely interested in getting to know you, he will rise to the level of your standards or lose interest. The reason why the writer felt powerless to effect any change in this situation is because she had already begun to settle. She had already given up too much to start over. When it comes to men and standards you rarely get a do over, so you have to get it right the first time. It is kind of like changing the rules of a game once the game has already started. This is why it is so important to have your non negotiables/must haves. I spoke about this more in my previous book, "The Dating Game: How to Find Yourself While Looking For Mr. Right." If you know you require good communication, quality time, romance, dates, chivalry, etc., do not allow yourself to sacrifice things you require. What good is being in a relationship if it is not a fulfilling one? What good is having a man if that man is not giving you what you need? Get what you need and want from your relationship; this is not just about having a warm body there or having someone to take you out so you have a reason to get all dolled up. If you are dating with the intention of being in a serious relationship, you are dating with a purpose. Time is the most precious commodity. You simply cannot afford to waste 5, 10 or even 20 years of your youth and vitality on an indecisive man. A man that is unable to make up his mind about you deserves to be nothing more than an option. As the saying goes, "Never allow someone to be a priority when they are making you an option."

If you feel like the man you are interested in is giving you mixed signals, he is probably not interested. Boys play games. Men, however, are upfront and straight forward if they are interested in you. You should never have to question a man's interest or intentions towards you if he is into you. If you feel confused on where you stand, unsure of what you mean to him or unclear about the direction your relationship is going, you may be a place holder. Ouch! I know that sounds harsh. No one wants to be a seat filler when you deserve to play the lead role. A man giving you mixed signals is keeping his options open. For whatever reason, he has not seen enough in you to want to invest fully in pursuing a relationship with you. That does not mean there is something wrong with you. Do not forget every man you date is not going to be "the one." The problem is not that you two aren't soul mates and meant to spend the rest of your lives together; the problem is he has lead you on to believe it is a possibility, knowing full well that it is not, at least on his end. Men send women mixed signals all the time for a variety of reasons. Here are a few:

He craves attention. Women aren't the only ones who like feeling wanted and desired. It is a huge ego boost for a man to know someone wants him, especially when the woman wants him so badly she is willing to lower standards or alter her beliefs just because he wants her to. He may be immature or enjoying the bachelor lifestyle too much to give it up for anyone but "the one." He could have trust issues. Men have baggage too. He may have been cheated on or lied to in the past and he's not willing to be vulnerable at the risk of it happening again. Another reason a man may be sending you mixed signals is because he feels he is too young to settle down. In his mind, he does not want to get married until he is at least 30, so when he meets you at 25 (despite how amazing you are) he feels like you are asking for too much. If he is interested but not ready to commit, he may say what it takes

to keep you around to buy him some time, but he will not be
pressured by your timetable or biological clock. The biggest
and most obvious reason he is sending you mixed signals is
because he wants to be intimate with you. Most decent
women are not interested in a casual romp in the sheets so to
make you feel a bit more respectable, he pretends it is more
than that. He pretends there are actual feelings involved. He
will play the role of your pseudo boyfriend as long as it suits his
needs. So, like the player that he, is he may check on you
periodically just to make sure you are still interested and he
still has you right where he wants you. This is why the
conversations are brief and shallow. He may offer the standard,
"How was your day?" question. You barely give him an answer
before he makes up some excuse to cut the conversation short.
You have convinced yourself you are in an actual relationship,
but he doesn't call himself your man or (like the writer of the
letter I spoke of earlier in this chapter) he does not call at all.
Men who send women mixed signals do it in a variety of ways;
some are obvious, but some are more subtle and more difficult
to detect. For example, when you are alone with him you are

the center of his universe. He is attentive, sweet and charming, but the minute you step foot out of the bedroom or his apartment he's different. He is not interested in introducing you to his friends and family. If he does he may refer to you as his "friend." He avoids meeting your friends and family because he doesn't want to be fully incorporated into your life and he does not want you fully incorporated into his. Be leery of men who would attempt to keep your relationship secret. Do not allow him to give you excuses like, "It's nobody's business what we have" or "We don't need titles to define what we are to each other." I cannot tell you how many times I have heard this from women over the years. Never let a man who is supposed to be with you allow himself to appear single, whether it's on social media or in real life. You are no man's dirty little secret, so don't allow him to treat you like one. Another reason men send mixed signals is because they like to feel powerful and in charge of every situation. He may want to move at his own pace. Some women do not mind pressuring a man into a relationship by asking repeatedly for a commitment, but men do not like feeling told what to do even if they were already going to do it. He is the chaser, not the chasee, remember? It is a matter of him doing things in his own time. Some men find it quite emasculating when a woman tries to dictate the levels and stages of a relationship. He may withdraw partially or even completely if he feels like you would never allow him to take some control. He could be sending you mixed signals because he doesn't know what he wants. We always believe that a man is self assured and knows exactly what he wants. That is not always the case, especially when it comes to matters of the heart.

Are we giving men too much credit here? Let them tell it they're not sending mixed signals or they're not sending signals at all. Whether it was his intention to confuse you regarding where you stand with him or not, he still did. Beware of the signs.

They don't call it a woman's intuition for nothing. Psychological studies have proven women are far better than our male counterparts at deciphering things like facial expression, body language and tone. They say women are better at deciphering subtle messages. When all else fails, go with your gut! Do not ignore the red flags or the tiny little voice inside you that once whispered gently, "Something's not right about him" but is now screaming it at the top of its lungs, saying, "Go! save yourself!"

CHAPTER SIX

How to Go From Wife Material

to Wife

There is nothing like the love of a good man. While I do not believe that a man can complete you, I fully believe he can compliment you. Depending on who you ask, men are the ones who do the choosing. I know for a fact that is not true. How many men have approached you in your lifetime? How many of those men did you actually give a chance? Men would like to think you just couldn't resist his good looks and charm. That is a huge boost to their ego, but it is not true. You spotted him long before he made his approach. Before he even opened his mouth, you had already decided whether you would or would not entertain him. We know how to give a man the brush off if we are not interested, and we know how to be flirty and coy if we are. The choice is yours. Peaking a man's interest is one thing, maintaining it is another thing entirely. The key is to make him want you without even looking like you are trying. Would you date you? There are several ways to make yourself the ultimate catch. Be confident. That is easier said than done these days. Now that we are in the age of social media everyone is putting their best photo shopped and filtered foot forward. Not too long ago, my husband and I were on a beach. My husband asked me, "Do you see any Instagram bodies out here?" His question took me off guard momentarily. I took a good long look around and said, "You know what? No I don't." "Exactly!" He replied. It's human nature to compare yourself to others, but comparison is the thief of joy. Just remember you, just the way you are, are someone's exact type. Some men prefer curvy plus sized women, petite women, women with natural hair, dark skinned women, flat-chested women, women who change their hair every other week etc. You have to know with complete certainty you can hold your own next to anyone. When you truly know that, you walk with your head high, your back straight and you own it! That confidence is what attracts men. You don't have to be the prettiest, the smartest or even the sexiest; you just have to know you are amazing and you carry yourself as such. There is a reason why iconic fashion houses like Gucci, Louis Vuitton, and Prada do not have commercials. They don't have commercials because they are Gucci, Louis Vuitton and Prada. Everyone knows they are high quality brands, so they don't have to advertise that. What is understood does not have to be explained. When you carry yourself as a confident woman with standards, it will be understood that only the customer willing or capable of rising to those standards will have a chance with you. Becoming wife material while you are single eliminates the need for on the job training. Use this time of singleness to find yourself and discover what you want out of life and a potential life partner. To attract the ultimate catch you must first *be* the ultimate catch. In this chapter, I will show you how to do just that.

Be a good listener. Whether it is your first date or your fifty year wedding anniversary, never stop listening. A common misconception is men do not express themselves. Although they may not be as vocal about their feelings as women, take note of his actions, facial expressions and body language. He may be a man of few words, but that does not mean he does not express himself in other ways. You don't have to nag or pry to get him to open up to you. Learn how to communicate with him in his love language. Perhaps you realize he tends to get really quiet when he is upset. You don't have to constantly ask him, "What's wrong?" You could just say something like, "It looks like something is bothering you. I don't want to push, but if you do want to talk about it I'm here. Even if you just want to vent." And then give him his space. If and when he does come to you, just listen. Men are not looking for you to solve their problems for them; they just want a non judgmental ear to listen. Men are taught when they are young boys to be tough and not show emotion because that makes them look weak. So, when he is trying to open up with you and share his innermost feelings, allow him to do so without ridicule or judgment. It takes a lot for a man to be emotionally vulnerable around a woman. Some men are unable to open up to you because their feelings for you are so strong they scare him.

Acknowledge him. If you want to go on a full on tirade about how all men are dogs there will be a long list of women ready to chime in and cosign your sentiments. However, you may receive as enthusiastic an endorsement for good men. Be the exception. If you have a great guy, do not be afraid to acknowledge that both privately and publicly. Some women are afraid to do this because they believe by broadcasting what a great guy they have it may draw the attention of other women. But, the key is being vague yet complimentary. For example, "I'm so thankful for the weekend my lovely boyfriend planned for me. Thanks babe". He may blush nervously and feign pseudo embarrassment over the gesture, but he secretly appreciates that you acknowledge him. Men love knowing they have satisfied you and made you happy. Pleasing a woman is an intensely gratifying feeling for them. They always want to feel like no other man could have done what they did for you or made you feel how they made you feel.

Be a one man woman. A man wants to know he can trust you around other men whether he is there or not. There is nothing wrong with being friendly and getting to know his friends and family, but never allow the interaction to cross the line. Men value loyalty. He needs to be confident that whether he is in your presence or not you are conducting yourself as a taken woman.

Incorporate yourself into his life. Make yourself hard to live without. This is not a hostile takeover so practice subtlety. Do those little things for him that allow him to get comfortable and used to you being around. Suggest the perfect gift for his mother on Mother's Day, make a big deal about his birthday, leave love notes in his car, take care of him when he's sick. This is all based on the fact that he deserves this and he is reciprocal in his treatment towards you. Basically, be thoughtful and put your imprint on every area of his life. Establish inside jokes, have an "our song," win over his family, friends and co-workers. I'm not saying leave your toothbrush and feminine products at his place. I'm talking about leaving him with an overall feeling that his life is incomplete without you. Be the woman he compares every other woman to. If you can successfully do this, you may elevate your status from wife material to wife. Make yourself irreplaceable and you won't be replaced. Remember men want women they believe add value to their lives. Constantly add to your relationship equity by investing in your relationship and, more importantly, in him. Position yourself to be the one he can depend and rely on by being there for him consistently.

Do not be afraid to disagree. Call him out if he says or does something you do not agree with. Some women believe the way to a man's heart is to be a "yes" woman who constantly strokes his ego and laughs at all his jokes (even ones that are not funny). In reality, men want a balance. They want a partner who is willing to allow them to lead. Men are more likely to be intrigued by you when you speak your mind without being condescending and insulting, but articulate and passionate. I am not recommending you start fights and become argumentative because you think it will get you the guy. Here's an example of what I mean. If he makes a statement like,

"...because everyone knows Biggie Smalls was hands down the best rapper ever." If you disagree, your rebuttal may be something like, "Does everybody really know that? I actually believe Tupac Shakur was the best ever! Tupac's "All EyezOn Me" album was a classic!" This may spark a playful banter with you both making your cases for why you believe you are right. There should be a mutual respect for each other's opinions. You should be able to have a difference of opinion without name calling and insults. If he values you and believes you are intelligent (even if he disagrees), he will at least consider your opinion. Much like the President of the United States surrounds himself with highly intelligent advisors to offer him perspective. Likewise, most men are interested in a woman who has her own opinions and values and knows how to express herself passionately without undermining him as man. This is how you separate yourself from other women and present yourself to be a challenge. A strong man needs a strong woman.

Be the occasional damsel in distress. Every uber feminist, "I don't need a man" and "I can do it on my own," type of woman reading this book may be outraged by this notion, but before you dismiss it entirely, hear me out first. Men love feeling like they solved a problem for you or used their masculinity to assist you (the fairer and 33% physically weaker on average sex) with a task or problem. Whether you require his assistance for small things like reaching a jar from the top shelf in your kitchen or getting out of his cozy bed in the middle of the night in the pouring rain to help you change a flat tire because you are scared and stranded on the side of the road, he wants you to ask for his help. Years ago, when my husband and I were dating, my car broke down. I didn't have much money so I was devastated when the mechanic gave me his estimate to repair my car. My husband, boyfriend at the time, told me the repairs I needed were not that complicated and he could do it. He had no more knowledge of cars and auto mechanics than I did, but he bought books and assured me he had taught himself how to complete the repairs. He spent hours upon hours in the hot sun for nearly a week with the auto mechanics book in one hand and a wrench in the other. When he was done he confidently told me to test drive it by taking it around the block. I barely made it down the street before white smoke began billowing from under the hood and the car slowed to a screeching halt. Although his attempt was unsuccessful, the idea that he put so much time and energy trying to be my hero was incredibly sweet and flattering to me. Men appreciate the demonstration of vulnerability and fragility it takes to allow them to help you. Although his wrench was clearly in the wrong place, his heart was not. Men love being surrounded by your feminine energy. It makes them feel more masculine and reaffirms their worth to you.

Give him some space. When you are interested in a man and you are trying to get to know him, it is natural to want to spend as much time with him as possible. Spending quality time with him confirms your interest, but demanding or making constant requests for his time can come across as a bit needy. Most men fear a needy woman the most. It is not that men are afraid to be in a committed relationship with a woman whose company they enjoy, but they are reluctant to give up their freedom. Men want women who have busy and fulfilling lives of their own. They want to know you are comfortable enough in your own skin to do things on your own. No one wants to feel tied down, thus the phrase, "the old ball and chain." If you are in a committed relationship with a man you trust, encourage him to spend time with his friends and have a life outside of your relationship. When he goes out with his friends to watch the big game or play basketball at the park, give him a little kiss on the cheek and say something like, "I'll miss you, but have fun." And, when he is out with his friends, avoid calling to check up on him. Demonstrate you trust him and you are not trying to interfere with his guy time. Better yet, make some plans of your own. You have an amazing and incredibly fulfilling life of your own. The key is to allow him to feel needed without you looking needy. You were getting along just fine before meeting him, so continue to thrive and flourish in your own journey of self-discovery. This journey does not end merely because you now have a significant other. You are fully capable of having a good time without him, just as he is fully capable of having a good time without you. As the saying goes, "Absence makes the heart grow fonder."

Believe in him and his dreams. Be honest with yourself about the possible reality of those dreams as well. If you don't genuinely believe in them, don't pretend to just for the sake of garnering more favor in his eyes. Do whatever you can to help him reach his highest level of potential. When I first met my husband, he was working at a summer camp making a little over minimum wage. It was not that he lacked education. In fact, he had earned his Bachelor of Science degree in Computer Information Technology. He would be the first to admit he struggled with writing his resume because he had no work history to speak of. Most of the positions he applied for turned him down due to lack of experience. I happened to be amazing at writing resumes and interviewing. At the time, I was an instructor at a college and part of my job was conducting mock interviews with my students and helping them with their resumes. I offered to work on his resume and practice interviews with him. He graciously accepted. He was working a well paying entry level job in his field within a matter of months. He was earning exponentially more money with his new position. He had already done the hard part; I just saw his tremendous potential and helped him to realize it. He tells me all the time that his love for me is what drove him to want more and to be more. When a man really loves you, he will (of his own volition) strive to be the man you deserve and he will love you for helping him reach that level.

Establish and maintain hobbies, interests and even friendships of your very own. You never want to completely lose yourself and your own personal identity in someone else. I often see women completely ditch their girlfriends the minute they are in a new relationship. Being in a relationship should not be the death of your single life. Yes, you have handed in your player card, but what does that have to do with the life you were living before becoming involved with someone else? If you love singing and you have been in your church choir for years, don't stop singing. If you enjoy reading in a quiet corner of your favorite bookstore on Sunday mornings with a nice tall cup of seriously over priced coffee, continue doing that. Two individuals make up a relationship so don't lose your sense of individuality.

Keep your options open. Unless there has been an official conversation, not an implied one, about being exclusive, you should still be entertaining other interested men. Men have no problem doing this whatsoever, but women sometimes tend to feel guilty about it. It does not matter how much he may act like your boyfriend, if he has not asked you to be your boyfriend you are still single and unattached. I know it is hard sometimes if you really like a guy to go on dates with men you may not like as much, but it keeps you from overinvesting and getting too attached in a non committed relationship. A man should always feel like your options are just as open as his are. Say for example you met him online on one of those popular dating websites and, after a few dates, he asks you to take down your dating profile. Do not agree to that unless it is a mutual decision that you both take down your profiles. Exclusivity is a privilege that is earned. If he is not willing to demonstrate how committed he is to this relationship, you should continue to date other men. When an interested man realizes there is a chance you could leave him for someone else, he will step up his game. Commitment is never a problem for a man who is genuinely interested. Relationships are not nearly as difficult as people make them out to be. They are only difficult when someone is not fully committed. If you feel like you have to pressure him, guilt trip him or give him ultimatums for him to be exclusive with you, you are wasting your time. A man will commit when he is good and ready, and not a moment before.

Let him miss you sometimes. Go out with your girlfriends. Heck, go out with your guy friends too. Do not spend your Friday and Saturday nights waiting by the phone or keeping your schedule clear just in case he calls. Do not be afraid to ask him, "I would love to go out with you, but I've already made plans. Can I have a rain check?" or "It's girls' night out tonight. What about tomorrow night?" To ensure he does not start thinking you are uninterested, always offer alternative date suggestions. Doing this lets him know that although you are interested in him, you are still your own person and you are not so afraid of losing him that you drop anything and everyone whenever he calls. This reinforces you are a quality woman. I remember when I first met my now husband. He asked me out on a date and I told him I could not go because I was planning on watching the NBA finals. My favorite team was competing for the championship. He laughed and asked, "So you're blowing me off for a basketball game?" I said in a flirtatious way, "Oh come on now. Don't be like that." I giggled. I could almost hear him smiling on the phone. He then suggested another date and time and I graciously accepted.

Everything is not always on his terms. A confident woman is not afraid that by doing this she will lose an opportunity with a great guy; she knows if she does, there will be another. A great way to see if he is still interested in you is for you to fall back a little and see if he rushes in to pick up the slack. If you text him, does he text you back within 24 hours or, better yet, does he call you?

Always bring your "A" game. On your first date, your mission is to get a second date if you are interested in him. This is not necessarily when you are trying to determine if he would make an amazing life partner or father to your unborn children. If this isn't your first date and you've been out with him already, be sure to remind him of what he has been missing. Look your best, engage him in thought provoking conversation and be flirty. This is when you want to express your femininity. Avoid over sharing and the urge to fill dead space or that awkward silence. A great conversation is like verbal tennis. The ball is in your court then his then yours again and... you get the drift. Remember, there is a fine line between appearing shy and appearing boring, so you may want to practice the art of conversation. It is okay to talk to strangers, whether it is the waitress, the cab driver, or the woman next to you at the doctor's office. Do not make the conversation all about you; make it about them, too. Find out what they are passionate about and the conversation will flow. Be genuinely curious. Let him learn more about you, but do it gradually. There's nothing wrong with being an open book, just allow him to read one chapter at a time. There should always be an air of mystery that surrounds you. You don't have to give him your complete autobiography on the first date. Reserve some things for the second date, third date or even first year of marriage. After an amazing date, allow sometime to pass and let him wonder what you are doing. He will likely start to think, "I wonder if she's seeing someone else."

Be his escape. Positivity goes a long way in dating. Men do not want to come home to a woman who is complaining constantly about her boss, her co-workers, traffic, gas prices, the news etc. Would you? When a man is considering if you would be a suitable life partner, he is thinking about what life would be like with you in the long run. Are you easily depressed? Are you needy? Do you have body issues and need constant reassurance? Is it exhausting just to be around you? If you are honest with yourself and these questions are true for you, you need to work on those issues, not just for your future mate, but also for yourself. A man wants his woman to be able to see the glass as half full as opposed to half empty all the time.

Let's say he takes you out to dinner at a new restaurant and the whole thing's a disaster. You almost miss your reservation because the parking lot is a nightmare, the waiter is ridiculously slow and he completely mixes up your order. However, the red velvet cake you order for dessert is absolutely delicious. You tell him with a smile something like, "I think this dessert saved the day. Here, have a bite." And you offer him a bite on your fork (if you're not a complete germaphobe that is). The ability to adapt and adjust will be useful throughout your relationship. He will see this as a strength. He may even think if some sort of crisis arises in the future he will know he can count on you to find the silver lining. That is a characteristic that can prove to be invaluable and may set you apart from other women he has dated in the past. If he is thinking long term, these are the kinds of personality traits he may be looking for without even knowing it. You want the relationship to flow as effortlessly as possible. Is this to say you should never express yourself honestly to a man? Absolutely not. However, you do not want to come off as someone who is always complaining, unhappy or constantly needs cheering up.

Have realistic expectations for your mate and your relationship. I blame Walt Disney and their countless Cinderella type movies for instilling this fairytale idea of love in young girls. Truthfully, love is not always rainbows and unicorn dust; it is work. One of my favorites movies is the 1997 film, "Love Jones" starring Larenz Tate and Nia Long. In this movie, one of the characters says, "Anybody can fall in love; falling in love ain't sh**. But somebody please tell me how to stay there." Forgive the crude language but reflect upon the statement as a whole. Falling in love is the easy part; maintaining and cultivating that love is what requires the work. We are in the age of social media and the temptation to over share our lives is too much for some people especially when they are head over heels in love. How often do you see posts of people who are fighting with their mate, not speaking to each other, or contemplating divorce? It's rare. The reason why we are often shocked and, in some cases, feel blindsided when one of our favorite couples (whether we know them personally or a celebrity couple we admired) breaks up or is headed for divorce is because the image they portrayed was only part of the story. And, we thought we knew them. There will be times when you disagree about trivial or inconsequential things, but if you want to increase the chances of a long relationship, you will have to become skilled in the art of compromise. Sometimes you win the battle and you lose the war, but you live to fight another day. You have to decide if being right all the time is more important than being fair and open to new perspectives.

Maintain your boundaries. He should not have a toothbrush at your place, clothes in a drawer, or his Xbox set up in your living room. He should not be comfortable coming over to your place every day unannounced if he is not in a relationship with you. He should not be expecting intimacy from you or planning to spend the night. Make it clear to him that access to your body is completely off limits. He is not allowed to get too touchy feely with you either. Blurring the lines will only confuse him and make him feel like there is no difference between being in a committed relationship with you and just "hanging out." Make the distinction crystal clear. It is like entering into a competition. Why would you compete as hard as you possibly could if they hand out trophies to everyone no matter where they placed? There should be certain parts of you emotionally and physically that only the man who has committed to you can access. Some men are with women because they are reliable. Every time he calls, she is there. Every time he wants to come over to her place, she says "yes." When he is not with her, he is actively pursuing other women because she never defined the relationship or demanded he adhere to any standards. Always present yourself as a challenge. A man should feel like your standards were put in place long before him and will remain long after him. For example, it is not just that you will not kiss him on the first date, but you will not kiss any man on the first date. Do not worry about scaring men off with your standards. It sets you apart from other women and, depending on what he is looking for, could solidify you in his mind as wife material. Men love challenging women because it demonstrates you are self assured and confident. It confirms you are not seeking validation from him or anyone else for that matter. What you are really saying to a man when you remain steadfast to your standards is, "I know what I bring to the table and I'm sure if you don't see my value someone else will." Men instinctively have a desire to chase, so let them. It is you who ultimately determines who catches you anyway. Even men with the best intentions will test your boundaries in an attempt to qualify or disqualify you as a potential life partner. The key in determining his intentions is to gauge how he responds to you when you enforce your standards. For example, if he invites you over to his place to watch Netflix and assures you, prior to you agreeing, there will be no sexual advances made, yet he relentlessly attempts to seduce you. He is testing you. If you give in to his advances, he may no longer take you seriously. This could potentially jeopardize his view of you. But, if you are firm in declining his advances and make it clear what will and will not be happening, he may let out a bit of a smirk and apologize profusely, but he will be on his best behavior. You'll get the feeling you've earned his respect, but you really just passed one of his tests. Earning a man's respect is not something you passively request, but something you demand. Upholding your standards is a lot easier than you may think. It is simply a matter of making your *shoulds* into your *musts*. Instead of saying, "He should call me on the phone instead of texting me all the time," say, "He *must* call me as opposed to strictly texting." Instead of saying, "He should love me just the way that I am," say, "He *must* love me as I am." Doing this does not just change a single word; it changes a mindset.

Do not play hard to get, *be* hard to get. There is a song by R&B group Brownstone called, "If You Love Me" and it should be every single woman's dating philosophy:

"If you love me, say it

If you trust me, do it

If you want me, show it

If you need me, prove it"

One of the common mistakes women make in dating is assumption. In your head you have this understanding about where things are going and what you mean to each other but, in reality, there has never been a formal discussion. I can't tell you how many women have written me letters brokenhearted because they realized they've been in a relationship all by themselves. They have been committed and exclusive with this man who has been dating other women the entire time. Is it his fault? Yes, but only partially. As immature and deceptive as it may be, some men will never tell you if you never ask. How do you avoid such deception? Ask the right questions early on to help you identify potential deal breakers. Never attempt to change his mind. Make sure both his words and his actions are aligned. Women with standards make no apologies for demanding more for a relationship because they know they are worth it. No free samples! If a man does not make it clear that he wants to take your relationship to the next level, a confident woman cuts her losses no matter how into him she may be and walks away. Not because she wants to, but because she has to. The longer you stay with a man who refuses to honor your standards, the less he feels like he has to. Your words have to match your actions too. Make him work for it. As the song lyric goes, "If you need me, prove it." Make sure you see he is actively putting in the effort to be with you and take your relationship to the next level. Men find value in anything (or anyone) they have to work for. Commit only to someone who is willing to prove he can be committed to you as well. Why chase him when you are the catch?

CHAPTER SEVEN

Men Can't Handle Strong Women:

Fact or Fiction

You are an attractive, intelligent and accomplished woman who has done quite well for herself, but you are still single. You have managed to succeed and even excel in every other area of your life, but when it comes to love, you have not figured that out yet. Is it that men are intimidated by you or is it that you come across as arrogant because of your accomplishments?

Are you sabotaging your own relationships? Before you quickly answer "no" as a knee jerk reaction, answer the questions posed below:

-Do you have a hard time telling a man (or anyone else for that matter) you need him?

-Do you *have* to have the last word?

-Do you prefer to do things on your own, that way you know it will be done right?

-Do you secretly enjoy arguing?

-Do you have a hard time taking/making and keeping friends?

-If you make more money than a guy do you think that means you are in charge?

-Do you feel like you make much better decisions than everyone else?

-Have you ever been told you are too controlling?

-Do you consider yourself a diva or think you deserve to be spoiled?

Still not sure if this sounds like you? Let's try a few scenarios.

It's your six month anniversary with your boyfriend and he takes you to the best restaurant he can afford. You do not particularly like the food or the service there. Would you:

a. Lie and tell him you love it there.

b. Make the most of it because he tried, but later tell him you do not really like that place.

c. Tell him to go somewhere else without even going inside.

d. Demand he take you somewhere else but offer to treat.

Your boyfriend makes you dinner. In the process he leaves the kitchen a wreck and the food is disgusting. Would you:

a. Pretend it is delicious and eat it anyway and clean the kitchen.

b. Take a few bites and give him a kiss for effort. Tell him you will order the pizza and help him clean the kitchen.

c. Take one bite and spit it out and, without even saying a word, begin cleaning up and cooking something else.

d. Tell him the food is disgusting, scold him for making a mess of the kitchen and demand that he clean it.

For your birthday, your boyfriend buys you a dress to wear on a date. It is definitely not your style. Would you:

a. Wear it once and then pretend you lost it.

b. Thank him, but tell him you already had the perfect dress in mind. Ask him if he would be offended if you returned it.

c. Secretly return the dress for one you want.

d. Tell him you pick out your own clothes.

You have been waiting for a month for the latest Idris Elba movie to come to theaters. Your boyfriend asks you to a movie to see another film. Would you:

a. See the movie he chose since he is the man.

b. Tell him you could see his movie this weekend and your movie next weekend.

c. Suggest an all nighter and see both movies.

d. Demand to see your movie and refuse to go if you do not get your way.

It's raining outside and your date offers to pull the car up front. Would you:

a. Think that is so romantic and wait for him to pull the car around.

b. Tell him you will race him to the car and giggle like a schoolgirl the whole way.

c. Tell him your hair is natural so it does not matter if it gets wet.

d. Tell him you are fully capable of walking to the car in the rain.

If you answered D to those questions you are a handful Miss Thing! Seriously, if you did answer D to most of these, you may be the reason why you are unable to establish and or maintain a new relationship. The phrase, "I don't need a man" has most likely been said on every continent and in every language. We have all been there. You know you are a catch. You are smart and funny, you have your own home and car, you make a great living etc., but you cannot seem to find a decent guy. You think to yourself, 'Men just can't handle a strong woman.' This is the go-to excuse of women with strong personalities who are unable to initiate, cultivate or maintain a meaningful relationship with a man. Is there any truth to this? Well, yes and no. Men do love strong women. In fact, most men find a self-assured and confident woman to be a turn on. However, when a woman is so strong minded that she exudes too much masculine energy, a man may become turned off. Most men view "strong minded women" as anti men. Masculine and feminine energy is a very delicate balance. To put it bluntly, men need women to make them feel like a man and women need men to make us feel like a woman. We are fully capable of carrying own bags, killing a spider or opening that incredibly stubborn jar of mayonnaise, but men like to do those things for us. It makes them feel needed. One of the biggest turn offs for a man is when a woman makes him feel like there's nothing he can do for her. When a man feels unable to provide for her mentally, emotionally, financially, sexually, etc., it emasculates him and makes him feel inadequate. When a man starts having these types of feelings, he may become more vulnerable to finding that sense of worth elsewhere. When men cheat, it is not always because the other woman is more attractive. In most cases, she is not. However, what the other woman did for the man that his woman did not was give him a sense of value and validated his contributions as a man. She allowed him to take care of her. Men have a fundamental need to provide. This isn't the fifties and the sixties. Men aren't the only ones bringing home the bacon. As women, we had to scratch and claw our way to get to where we are in the business world. We now have supervisory and managerial positions. We are entrepreneurs and CEOs of multi-million dollar companies. In the corporate world, we have to be tough to ensure we are not taken advantage of, belittled or discriminated against solely based on our gender. We are often in hostile work environments that are cut throat and force us to keep our guards up. Showing vulnerability at work could be seen as weak and unprofessional, so we have conditioned ourselves to mask our emotions, especially around men. We often take this aggressive attitude with us even once we have left our workplace. We take this attitude with us on our dates and it is still there when we start a new relationship. The problem is not that women should not be strong, intelligent and have their own mind and views on the world. The problem is that you must allow a man to exert his masculine energy and not feel like it is competing with yours. Men want you to ask them to help you bring in the groceries, borrow his coat if you are cold or insist that you not drive your car because the back tires need to be replaced. They want to feel as if you need them to help you solve a problem. I know this is making every feminist reading this book want to burn it, but hear me out. What you offer a man with your feminine energy is just as important to him. Men love to see a woman expressing her softer side. This is not about you pretending to be weak or inferior. This princess doesn't need saving remember? This is about you allowing him to take care of you, not because you can't take care of yourself, but because you realize this is his way of showing you his love and affection. It does not matter if a man is making minimum wage or a six figure salary; he still wants to be treated and looked upon as a provider. Even if you are in a position where you are making more than a potential suitor, allow him to show you he can provide for you in other ways. Allow him to be your confidant when you need some advice about how to handle a problem at work. Allow him to make some uncontested decisions in your relationship. As a strong-minded independent woman, you have a choice to make. You can either pursue relationships with passive "yes" men with no backbone, or you can allow a man to show you he can take care of you. By no means am I saying you should be submissive to all men. You should only be submissive to your husband and him to you. Men love to show you they can be a "take charge" kind of guy, so let him take charge. It is not a matter of whether you are capable of doing things for yourself; it is a matter of you being capable of allowing him to do it for you, thus, satisfying his need to prove his masculinity to you. In doing so, you are not relinquishing your power and admonishing your independence to soothe the fragile ego of a man. You are still operating from a position of power while celebrating and embracing your own femininity.

Most strong-minded women claim that they want a strong man, but you have to face a few facts. Would that type of man be interested in a woman who doesn't allow him to exert his masculine energy? Men crave feminine softness. A man does not want to be with a woman exuding the same masculine energy he is. He is looking for an opposite. You can show a man your vulnerable and softer side without being dependent and needy. This is about balance. You can dominate in the boardroom, but when you are around your man you can allow him to give you a foot massage, make you dinner, run you a bubble bath or any other chivalrous act he has planned as a show of his affection. You have to understand it is okay to let someone take care of you. A man needs to know you feel safe with him, not just physically safe, but also emotionally safe... safe enough to be emotionally vulnerable and let your guard down around him. Yes, your resume is quite impressive and you should be proud of your career advancements, but a man interested in a relationship is not considering that. He is not hiring you for a position; he is evaluating you to see if there's chemistry, physical attraction and a deeper connection. Not one to mince words, I found this anonymous post on a relationship forum that read, "The only strong minded women men feel threatened by are the women who aren't INTELLIGENT enough to pick their battles wisely and assert themselves GRACEFULLY. If you as a woman are constantly beating a guy over the head, insisting that everything be YOUR way, and telling HIM how to think and feel, I'm not sure that even meets the true definition of "strong minded." Truly strong-minded women know when to stand their ground and when to NEGOTIATE. If a woman INSISTS on having her way in every little thing and screaming out HER opinions on every question, that is not "strong minded;" that's simply being a pain in the..."

Although what this gentleman said could have been said with more tact and decorum, I can appreciate his brutal honesty and candor. When a man hears a woman say, "Men can't handle me" or "Men are intimidated by a strong woman like myself," he runs as fast as he can in the opposite direction. You say you want a strong man, but you never allow him to exhibit that strength. A man does not want to be constantly challenged, belittled or undermined. Your mate is not the enemy, so don't treat him like one. Do not meet his suggestions with hostility and doubt.

I consider myself to be a shrewd business woman. To be successful it is necessary for me to be tough, negotiate and demand things be done a certain way. My husband of ten years has rarely seen that side of me. Unless he overhears me on a conference call or I ask his advice about a business deal, he has never dealt with my business persona. That is by design. I leave my business persona at the door when I am with my husband. He represents my safe place. When I am with him, he absorbs my stress. He allows me to rest in my femininity. Allow your man to express his masculinity and strength. Here's an example of how I do that. When I go grocery shopping, I call my husband when I am a few minutes away from home and ask him to come outside to help me with the bags. I know I am fully capable of bringing in the bags myself, but he loves that I leave the heavy bags for him. It seems like a small gesture, but it reinforces to him that I need him and it allows me to be dainty and fragile. I pretend to put up a fuss when he hands me the eggs and the bread, knowing I can carry much more than that. It feels amazing to have a big strong provider who is willing to come outside (even in his pajamas sometimes or in the rain) to make sure his lovely wife doesn't strain herself bringing in the groceries. My husband told me once, "I want the only thing you have to worry about is what you are making for dinner."Hallmark has nothing on my husband. That was one of the sexiest things a man has ever said to me. I am not suggesting you just give your trust to just any man. However, when the man you are with has shown you he loves, cherishes and respects you, and you are confident he has your best interests at heart, allow him to take some of the burden away from you. Consider it from his perspective. He works hard at his 9 to 5 job. He may have a manager and/or supervisor giving him instructions and assignments throughout the course of his day. He does not want to be in a relationship where you remind him of his boss. He wants to be able to make decisions. If you want to marry a man who is strong enough to be a leader, then you must be willing to be lead. Let me ask a question here. Do you feel you are too strong or are you too much of a control freak? The incessant desire to want to dictate or control every area of your life including your relationships could ruin every relationship you have, intimate or otherwise. It's likely you gradually became controlling because you trusted your heart to someone who broke it. So, as a defense mechanism, you demand to have full control of a situation. If you truly want love, allow him to love you in his own way. A strong woman is a lot like a turtle. She has this extremely tough outer shell, but inside she's just as soft and vulnerable as any other woman. She has just convinced herself that showing that side of her is a sign of weakness. It is okay to show that vulnerable side to the man you are with if he has earned that right. Not everyone gets to see that side of you. Not everyone should. It is something that should be special and help to forge a sacred bond between the two of you. You have to decide if you would rather be right all the time or be in a committed relationship because it may not be possible to have both. If a man feels you are special, he may try to deal with this issue and prove to you his intentions toward you are pure, and that he is not trying to take advantage of you. However, men are human, and as much as he would like to be with you, he won't do it at the expense of sacrificing his manhood or masculinity forever. It is unfair for you to ask or even expect him to. If the idea of letting someone else take control scares you, start small. Allow him to pick the movie or the restaurant for your date without questioning his choices. This is just a starting point. Once a man has earned your trust, you can feel safe enough around him to give him a bit more. It is a gradual process, but if he is patient enough and thinks you are worth it, he will try to help you figure this out. Don't take this for granted because you are expecting him to compromise quite a bit of who he is so you can become who you need to be. There is a great deal of sacrifice on his part. He wants to love you, so let him... in his own imperfect and sometimes flawed way. Am I suggesting you abandon who you are and take on this meek and mild persona that is nothing but a weak and watered down version of who you really are? Absolutely not. What I am saying is you do not have to prove how tough you are to him. If you cannot allow yourself to trust him and let your guard down around him (if he has earned it of course), your relationship with this man (or any other man for that matter) may be doomed from the start. This type of behavior demonstrates your own insecurities and trust issues. Insecure women are the exact types of women men try so desperately to avoid. As much as a man loves you, he could decide that it may require far too much time and energy to support you while you break down your emotional barriers. Most men are looking for women who are carefree, not women who are bullies, argumentative, controlling or demanding. As a life partner, he wants someone whose mere presence improves his quality of life, not someone who challenges him in every way. He does not want to feel like you are competing to climb the success ladder. Just remember, anything with two heads is a monster.

CHAPTER EIGHT

Paying for Dates

As we have already discussed in the previous chapter, we as women have come a long way in the business world. Many of us are self-assured, independent and financially stable. There is a quote I love that reads, "Don't let what he brings to the table be all you have to eat." Being a financial asset to your mate is a great thing. However, I believe that going Dutch on a first date is an absolute no-no! This letter I received from a young woman will assist me in making my point. It reads:

"Hello BronzeGoddess01. My name is _____ and I am a 22 year old college student. My major is psychology and I have the desire of becoming a child psychologist. In January, I met a guy who worked at the gym and we instantly connected. He was a college student as well studying the same major as I. On that night I met him, we exchanged numbers, and began texting ever since. Later, he recommended that we should go out on a date, we did, but he didn't pay. As months went by, we went on a couple more dates and he still DID NOT PAY. I also ended up meeting his friends and his family. His birthday came up and he payed for a hotel for the weekend and my stupid self ended up spending the weekend with him as well. We were not in a relationship, yet we acted like it. During his birthday weekend, he considered that he payed for our meal and that I payed for the movies. During that weekend we continued to go half on our dates. He once said to me "I like your maturity because you don't mind going half, my ex was a "DIVA" because I always had to pay, and that bothered me". A month later, he then "CONSIDERED" that we should go see a movie that I really didn't care for to see, but I went with him cause I wanted to spend time with him. Again, the movie was only $5 but he still didn't pay. A week later, I mentioned to him that as many times we been out on dates....YOU NEVER OFFERED TO PAY. Yes we were intimate, which I don't regret because I felt like it was a lesson learned. After I told him that, he apologized and said there will be a change and he didn't want it to seem like he was disrespecting me, and how much I was becoming a priority in his life. Unfortunately, there was no change. He asked me if I wanted to go out for chinese food and I said yes. He mentioned that this was a real date, and so I said, "do you mind picking me up?" He replied I don't mind, but you have to buy my marijuana if I do. That made me realize that he clearly doesn't recognize my self worth. Why should I have to buy your weed if you're picking me up and paying for my dinner? Idk if he wasn't raised in a way that a man is supposed to pay on dates, but I clearly didn't see it. As a woman, I don't mind pay for dates either, but he NEVER offered to pay during the 3 months that we were talking. I felt like he was all talk and no show. I talked to a couple of my guy friends about it and they considered that I deserve better and to LET HIM GO. I felt like God told me to leave him alone because he did not recognize my self worthand he is clearly not the one. After I sent him a looooong text saying that I am no longer interested in him, I also told him that he's been leaving bad impressions and I felt like he always wanted me to work around this time. He replied back that "If you feel like I should impress you then that's not what I'm going to do". Now he is trying to keep in contact with me and trying to hang out, but I am not giving him the time of the day. I am now just worried about my money, my education, and making myself happy. I also feel like God is now working on me to build a closer relationship with him. Do you think I did the right thing by leaving him alone? I know I did but I also want to know is there a limit to wanting a guy to do a lot for you and how do you get a guy to recognize your self worth?"

This letter is a prime example of how some men treat women who are so eager to date they do not allow a man to be a gentleman and properly pursue them. When the love interest in this letter said, "If you feel like I should impress you then that's not what I'm going to do," that was as crystal clear a sign that he is not worth your time as any other I have ever seen. As I mentioned earlier, you do not often get do-overs in dating, so you have to get it right the first time. This is not saying if you both are poor college students and you cannot afford very much that you should never go Dutch. If you are poor college students, avoid "hanging out" in his dorm room alone with him. That is not considered a date. Be leery of men who put little to no effort into spending time with you or who are extremely stingy with spending money on you. Men who always want you to come over to his place and "chill" are the worst ones. Unless there are actual activities planned, that is not a date. Allow him to express his creativity. You can still be romantic on a shoestring budget. Let me give you a personal example. When my husband and I first started dating, he was working a minimum wage job because he was not able to find a job in his field immediately following college. I was making quite a bit more money than he was at the time, but he still insisted on paying for the dates. Once we became a couple, I would sometimes treat him. He was always very uncomfortable about it, but I didn't mind because we were in a committed relationship. He would come up with creative dates that were still fun and romantic like picnics in the park, pizza and movie night (this was when video rental stores were at their peak) or poetry readings at a local coffee shop. My favorite movie is "Love Jones" with Larenz Tate and Nia Long, so this was right up my alley. We would get our $5 Little Caesars pizza and rent our video on 99 cents day and it was magical. I knew he was doing his best with what he had and, although our dates were not very fancy in the beginning, I knew he wanted to spend time with me, so I was still impressed. How a man treats you with regard to his money can be a very telling sign as well. The man in this letter made it seem almost as if she was lucky to be with him. Forget that it may sound old fashioned to you and you can well afford your own meal, movie ticket, popcorn etc. It is about the principle of the matter. When the writer of the letter paid for herself on the very first date and subsequent dates, she sent a very clear message to the man whether she knew it or not. She thought he would be impressed but, instead, I believe it was a turnoff to him. Men want to feel like they are providing for you. It is an insult when you make a man feel like there is nothing he can do for you, not even buy you dinner. From that moment on, I believe he started treating this "relationship" as more of a business transaction. The fact that she was intimate with him despite him treating her as if "he did not have to impress her" is why he is treating her a particular way. Let him pay for the first date. Don't even pretend to reach for your purse knowing full well you are hoping, wishing and praying he will say, "No no, I've got it," just so you can smile graciously and say in your best 'this is such a pleasant surprise' voice "Thank you for dinner." You are not being high maintenance or a "diva" as the man in the letter referred to the writer. It is not presumptuous of you to expect a man to pay because he was the one who asked you out. It would, however, be presumptuous of him to have planned the details of the date and assumed you were able to pay half. He should not have asked you out if he was incapable of paying for the date. When you ask how much dinner was or grab the check, it sends a message to the man that you may only be looking for friendship, or you may not feel like spending time with you is worth the cost of dinner, or you do not think he can afford to date you. In my opinion, it is a turn off and ill advised. When you are out to dinner or on a date with a man, the cost of the date *he* planned is none of your concern. The cost of dinner has not earned him any special privileges with you either. Never feel or allow someone to make you feel you must repay his generous gestures with some form of intimacy. He is owed nothing. Your body and your dignity is worth so much more than a steak dinner. Do not sell yourself short. I know you have had a great time. You thoroughly enjoyed the food, the ambience and conversation and you want to do this again sometime, so you offer to pay almost as an incentive for him to ask you out again, but you do not have to bribe or entice an interested man into spending time with you, so don't even attempt to do so. As demonstrated in the letter, feeling obligated to pay for his company gets very old very quickly. And don't you dare feel guilty about it either. It does not matter if you make more money than he does; it is about allowing him to show you with his money how interested he is in you. He is not buying you; he is demonstrating his interest.

Let him put his money where his mouth is. He says he cares for you and wants to get to know you better, then let him prove it. He *should* be trying to impress you and any man who does not feel like he has to is not worthy of you. Does he have any idea how many men there are out there who would love the pleasure of your company? Does he know how many men are vying for the opportunity to date you? Whether he is the only man pursuing you or not, the man you are casually dating should always feel like you have your options open, and that he is actually the man you have chosen out of all your suitors to spend the evening with. So, if he wants to be the only man you are spending time with he is going to have to work for it. If you do not get anything out of this book, please get this: make him earn everything! Now this is not the case for every man. There is a small but growing group of men who are impressed when a woman takes the initiative and pays for dinner. They may even find it sexy or even respectable. Dating is expensive! For men who are actively going out and pursuing women they could easily spend hundreds of dollars or more per year on dates.

Some women say chivalry is dead. Sadly, I believe gestures like this one are what killed it.

Here are a few statics on going Dutch you may find interesting. In 2013, ABCNews.com conducted the Fredrick Study to determine exactly who does and who should pay for dates. The study was made up of 17,000 straight unmarried participants between the ages of 18 and 65. According to the study:

-84% of men and 58% of women reported that men pay for most expenses after dating for a while

- 57% of women offered to pay but 39% of women wanted their men to reject the offer

- 44% of women were bothered when asked to pay

- 64% of men said that the women should contribute financially to a relationship

- 76% of men felt guilty when a woman paid

- 75% of men and 83% of women shared some dating expenses by the six-month mark

This is exactly why men say women are so difficult to figure out. We demand equal pay in the workforce, but we also want a chivalrous man to pay for dates. However, there are contradictions in this study coming from both sides. Men want women to pay, yet feel guilty when they do. They can't seem to make up their minds either. As a woman, your choices are your prerogative. You can hold onto your old fashioned values and still be a modern day woman. Either way, determining financial compatibility is an important step that cannot be ignored. You do not want to secretly resent your mate for making you pay for dates like the writer of this letter has begun to do. Does a man want you to contribute financially in a relationship? Yes. Should you do so right away and as early as the first date? No. In my opinion, once you are a couple and spending more and more time together, the lines of who pays for what can begin to blur and that is perfectly understandable. However, when you are dating someone new and still in the process of seeing if this relationship has the potential for something more, those lines should be a bit more defined. It is all about balance. Do not attempt to treat your dating life like a business transaction. The man pursuing you is not your future employer; he is a potential life partner, therefore, the rules of business do not apply here. Money is already an extremely touchy subject whether you have it or not. Avoid making money an issue. Having an awkward exchange over the check after an amazing date is the quickest way to ruin an extremely romantic and enjoyable evening. If he has asked you out, it should be understood that he should pay. If you pay for the first date, often times anxiety and maybe even a small sense of resentment begin to build. On the next date, you may be thinking, "I wonder if he expects me to pay again or was that a one time thing," or "Should I pretend to reach for the check when it arrives?"or "What will he think of me if I don't?"It is hard to just relax and enjoy the second date with these types of thoughts running through your mind. If he does not flinch when the check has been laid on the table or, even worse, slides it over to you, what do you do? What message would you be sending to him if you continue to pay for dates. Will it then be acceptable for you to start paying for him as well? He may think he is so handsome and so charming you have no issues paying to be in his company (which makes you seem a bit insecure by the way), and just like that the roles feel as if they have been reversed. Like the writer of the letter, you may begin to notice a decline in his desire to impress you, and you begin to resent him for it. The ugly truth of this is paying for dates is the same as buying his time. This makes you seem desperate. A man genuinely interested in you will not feel comfortable with you paying for dates. Regardless of how strong and independent you say you are, actions always speak louder than words. You can have a tremendous business acumen. You are a degreed professional moving your way up the economic ladder but, in the dating arena, you feel like paying for dates is what it takes to have a man want to spend time with you. The wrong man will see this as a sign of an insecure woman and exploit it for all it's worth. He will get as much out of you as you are willing to give. He may begin to escalate his requests. He may test you to see just how into him you are. This is why establishing financially compatibility and upholding certain standards is so important. Once you start compromising on what you know you deserve, you may have to continue doing so. As my mother once told me, "What you compromise to get, you must compromise to keep." Let me also say this, he cannot take you out on enough steak dinners, buy enough fancy things or treat you to enough of the most exotic getaways for him to imply or believe he deserves to have sex with you. If you are ever in a situation where you are on a date with a man and he asks or suggests that you pay for dinner and that makes you feel uncomfortable, motion for your waiter or waitress and ask them to create a separate bill with your charges and pay for your meal and allow him to pay for his. When it comes to dating and standards, there are no do-overs, so you have to get it right the first time. Establish your standards right away. Maintain them and reinforce them when necessary. This is not about playing games and this is not one of a million dating rules; this is about knowing your worth. Spending time getting to know you is worth the cost of the movie, dinner and then some.

CHAPTER NINE

Men to Avoid at All Costs

A bad guy does not seem so bad initially or you would never give him a chance. Slowly but surely, a man may reveal less than desirable personality traits, mannerisms, character flaws and idiosyncrasies. As a dating coach, I have received hundreds of letters from women of all different races, ages and economic backgrounds, and one thing remains the same. They ignored the warning signs. Not all of these women are naive and inexperienced; some just do not know what to look for. That is exactly what this chapter is about. Far too often, we do not realize who a man really is until we are head over heels in love with him. By then it is far too late. Before you begin investing your time and energy into a man, make sure he is worth getting to know. Here are some types of men you should avoid:

First, there is the player. I have already dedicated an entire chapter in this book to exposing the player and his methods, but I had to include it here as well. Players by definition have an insatiable appetite for women. So many women attempt to change this type of man. Stop me if you have heard this before. A good-looking man approaches you and attempts to get to know you. He has neglected to tell you he is already in a relationship. Most likely it is you who finds out he is involved with someone else. He tells you their relationship has been over, but he is just going through the motions. He does not love her anymore, but out of respect for the love they once shared, he does not want to hurt her. He tells you what he has with you is different. He wants you to give him a chance and give him some time to end his relationship. He continues pursuing you relentlessly, but never officially ends his relationship. He takes you on dates, calls you, spends time with you, etc., but it has been weeks, months or even years and he still has not ended that relationship. You have already invested so much time getting to know him and allowing him to get close to you. You do not want to end things because you feel like he will be free of his relationship at any moment. So, you wait...Gotcha! You have been played. Players always pretend to fall hard and fast for you. To avoid being played do the following: simply pull away when a man who is already attached to someone else tries to attach himself to you. Do not allow someone else's boyfriend, fiancé or even husband turn you into the other woman or a mistress. See it for what is really is and not better than it is. A man who is not mature enough to end his current relationship to pursue you is not romantic in any way. He will attempt to escalate the flirty conversations to a sexual one. Do not entertain his phone conversations, emails, texts, etc. If he is genuinely interested in you, he will end his current relationship properly. You do not want a man who will cheat so easily on someone else. If he will cheat with you, he will cheat on you. Do not let him play the victim. He will attempt to gain sympathy from you by portraying himself as the good guy who somehow got caught up in a bad relationship. Make it clear to him you are no man's second option, and if he wants to be with you he will have to prove it. Some men think their game is so good they can sell bottled water to a drowning man. Talk is cheap! Regardless of what he is saying, you are a woman of standards. Until he has ended his current relationship, he has chosen her. A relationship is only big enough for two people. There is simply no room for you in this one. Let him know you are not interested in sharing him with anyone and continue dating. Refuse to let this unavailable man waste your valuable time with his lies and empty promises. Do not wait for him to make a choice. You choose for him and take yourself out of the scenario. When you uphold your standards, you reaffirm your worth to a man and, more importantly, to yourself.

The serial dater. He's defined in the Urban Dictionary as one who engages in the process of systematically dating an obscene amount people in a short span of time. Not sure if this is your guy? Here are a few signs he may be: he's an older gentleman who has never been married. He says he wants to settle down and get married, yet he has never had a significant long term relationship. He disappears often and is constantly in and out of your life, and he loves to go out to clubs and bars with his friends. We spoke about this kind of man earlier. A man fully immersed in this stage of life is not ready for any type of serious commitment. He loves his bachelor lifestyle and he is not ready, willing, nor able to give it up. This is the type of man who seems to have everything going for himself – great career, nice house and car, amazing friends, and you wonder why such an awesome catch like this is still single... because he wants to be.

Then there's the Mama's boy. At first you think how close he is to his mother is incredibly sweet. Surely, a man capable of loving his mother this much can definitely love you too, right? Here's a letter I received from a woman in an uphill battle with her future mother in law:

"I have a soon to be MIL and a sis In law, well the entire family does not like me. Because they did not like the fact that I'm so quiet, they wanted me to open up and talk to them and social with them..sorry but that's just how I am. I'm a very quiet person, so the entire family doesn't like me since the start...fiancé and I been together for over 8 years and got engaged for a year. Last Saturday was supposed to be our big wedding day but we called it off a few months before the date. Yes because of this drama his entire family started, how everything became worst because the in laws asked me to speak my mind and let it out. They wanted to talk things out but during the conversation they disagree with one thing that I said and things got heated from there...my fiancé apparently thought I was talking back and I shouldn't have explain myself or said anything. He said that I should have just agreed and let them be right. Because he thinks that's talking back. He asked me to say sorry to them and so I refused...mind you guys I was already living with the in laws, few days later in that week I decided to move out and I called his mom said "I'm sorry I think it's best if I move out, I don't wanna bother the family and didn't mean to cause problems..moving out I think will be best for both" she replied back "you can move out and go wherever you want, he's my son he's staying" well what do you know? He stayed back and let me leave by myself, they said to him that if he move out too they will disown him. At the time he actually made me thought it was all my fault and that i shouldn't have explain myself or open up to the in laws...I actually thought things would have be better if I was to shut my mouth like I always did. Now I'm turning 30 and still not marry nor have kids. I'm so depressed and so disappointed....and this is the worst part, I'm still with him. Yep I'm an idiot...he is such a good person and a good friend but to me I don't know if he will be a good husband. He did not have my back since day 1 and up till this day, I still decided to have a wedding with him but this time will be a destination wedding, his response was "if we don't have blessing from my family if no one go I won't be happy and no point of having a wedding if my parents are not there, we should just do common law" wow I don't know how many more slap in the face for me to see this?? He said if you didn't act so rational or talk back everything would've been fine...wow. My families everyone said not to come back to him, but yet I'm still around. At times I wish to die and end it because I'm so confused."

Most mama's boys are raised by single mothers. She has never had to compete with anyone for her son's affection because she has always been the number one woman in his life. She considers you a threat, so she is intimidated by you. She seemed to like you at first but, for reasons unbeknownst to you, something changed or she never liked you (for whatever reason). She started demanding more and more of his time. You notice that she is making him choose between the two of you. Her approach to this could be subtle or blatant. For example, she might ask him to do something for her when she knows he has already made plans with you, or meddling in your relationship and offering unsolicited advice. You feel like she is sabotaging your relationship. She may still be friends with his ex or try to get them together behind your back. Even when she is caught red handed, your man refuses to acknowledge his mother is trying to ruin your relationship. Trying to get him to see he is being manipulated by his mother is an exercise in futility. Deep down he may know what his mother is doing but, to keep from making a tough decision, he turns a blind eye to the situation and does his best to let you two resolve your issue yourselves. Until a man like this has the courage to stand up for your relationship and demand that his mother respect the boundaries, you will be miserable in a relationship with him. In order for this to work, the two of you would have to represent a united front. Confronting his mother on your own will only make matters worse. If your man does not believe enough in your relationship to stand up for it and defend it, even to his mother, she will continue trying to destroy what you two have. Just as it says in the Bible in Mark 3:25, "A house divided against itself will not stand" (NIV). Love should be an opportunity and not an obligation. You deserve better than a man who is not strong enough to defend your love to his mother, his family or even the world if necessary. "For this reason a man will leave his father and mother and be united to his wife, and the two will become one flesh" (Matthew 19:5NIV). If he is unable to leave his mother physically or even emotionally, he is unwilling and unable to love you the way you deserve to be loved. A man should love and honor his parent, but if he wants to start a family with someone else, he must realize he must become his own man and not his mother's little boy. There comes a time in a man's life when he has to declare himself a man and carry himself as such. Unfortunately, there are some men well into their twenties, thirties and beyond who still are not ready to do that and some never will.

Sometimes it is not just his mother who stands in the way of your happiness; sometimes it is the entire family. When I am not writing books and coaching, I'm answering letters written to me by my YouTube subscribers. I once made a video answering a letter I received from a woman whose husband was threatening to leave her because she refused to let his unemployed brother move in with them in their new home. The couple had recently married and shared a child together. The brother had never had a job; in fact, his lack of financial stability was the exact reason he was going through a divorce and needing a place to stay. I completely fell in love with this comment left by one of my viewers:

"Ladies, this is why that whole "you're marrying him not his family" mindset is untrue. The writer could've figured all of this out just by being observant during the dating stages. With the holidays coming up ladies get in the kitchen where all the women are and sit back LISTEN and WATCH. See who is the moocher in the family....is your man the only one gainfully employed in this family? Will they look to him for money? Are there strong men around or are his uncles 60+ outside drinking talking about "these hoes ain't loyal? How many people are married in his family? What type of women are in his family...are they nurturing? Do they carry themselves with class? If you married into this family would you leave your kids with them ALONE? These are all things that need to come into play when women choose marry. It's never just him....it's his family too."

There is nothing wrong with a man who comes from a close knit family. Isn't that what we all want? However, there's a fine line between close and suffocating. In scenarios like this, the family often makes unrealistic and unfair demands on their loved ones. Those demands force the men to choose them or the woman in their lives. Beware of the warning signs. Be sure to study a potential mate's family dynamic before becoming romantically involved. Make sure you would be a good fit. Avoid trying to see the situation as it could be, and see it how it actually is. If nothing changed, could you live with his dynamic "as is?" Do not expect things to change once you marry a man or have children with him. As I often say, "Who you date is who you marry. You can't alter a man at the altar." When you notice a man's family is far too dependent on him for things such as money and time, take note of how often he obliges them. Does he often neglect you and your wants and needs for theirs? Do you notice they purposely make him choose? For example, does he cancel plans with you because they've made a request for his time? Are they constantly borrowing money from him? Has he taken on the father figure role to younger siblings? Does his mother treat him more as a boyfriend than a son? Has his family made any effort to welcome you into their family? In these types of scenarios, the family does their best to sabotage the relationship to ensure their loved one will be at their beck and call, just as he always has been. Try not to take it personally. It's not that they don't believe you are good enough for their loved one; they don't believe anyone is good enough for him. The more they see you as a threat, the more they resent you for what they perceive is you trying to steal their loved one away from them. Unless or until a man feels strongly enough for you to make you his number one priority and outline non-negotiable boundaries for his overbearing family, there is little hope that a relationship like this will survive. Now before you say you too are from a bad home and come from a dysfunctional family, please understand these are merely things to consider. We are all a product of our environment, but to what extent is completely up to the individual. This is where the spirit of discernment I spoke about earlier comes into play. If you are a believer, pray and ask God to reveal to you if this relationship is worth pursuing. Ask him to protect your heart from anything or anyone that means to harm you. This includes emotional harm as well.

Beware of a man who is insecure or intimidated by your success. The following letter is what typically happens in scenarios like this one:

"Hello,

My ex and I are high school sweethearts and dated for 8 years. He was a good boyfriend but lacked ambition and focus. He's a dreamer and I'm a pursuer. The more I thrived academically (won numerous scholarships and awards in college), the more insecure he became. Even though I never rubbed my success or education in his face, he always felt inadequate because he said he felt I "deserved better." He knows that some of mentors and family members want me to date someone more on my "level" and his bitter mother (his father left her for another woman) used to tell him that I would eventually leave him or cheat on him with someone in college or medical school. I ended up attending college out of state and his mom told him if I really loved him, I would have went to a local college, and this foolishness further fed into his insecurity. I have NEVER cheated on him nor gave him a valid reason to believe so, but yet he still feels insecure. I would think my ambition and determination would have rubbed off on him by now but unfortunately it hasn't. He didn't attend my college graduation due to his insecurities, which hurt me, and he ended up cheating on me with a girl woman who isn't on my level mentally, educationally, or physically. I don't understand how he could cheat on me with a 19 year old female who has no direction in life, and who physically and verbally abuses him and has a lot of emotional baggage. Where did I go wrong? I was loyal, faithful, beautiful and doing great things in life, AND even tried to help him pursue his goals, but it seems as if I was more determined for him to succeed than he was. I hear so many men, especially black men, complain about how difficult it is to find a non-ratchet black woman who is about something and have a good head on her shoulder. I would think he would have remained loyal got his life together to keep me around.

After years of false promises of "getting his life together," I started to lose respect and admiration for him and stop taking him serious when he talks about his life aspirations. He claims the new girl worships the ground he walks on and makes him feel like the best thing ever. He says he likes her because she believes in him and strokes his ego. He even claims that she told him that she feels he is the best should could do, Lol ! I don't know if she's delusional or he is, or if this is even true. I have no doubt that I could do better, I even have qualified men who wants to date me, but I always felt that since he and I been together so long and he was with me before I started succeeding in life, I feel as if I should try to help him succeed too. Maybe I was so invested in him because he was my first love and first and only boyfriend.

Fortunately, I have a lot of people who support my dreams and helped me succeed in life, and unfortunately, he doesn't have that support system. His bitter mother always tries to manipulate him by making him feel bad in order to get what she wants. For example, if she sees he is saving money for, let's say, a car or to move out, she would come up with some story for why she needs money, and when he says no, she tries to make him feel bad, which ultimately leads to him giving her money or what she wants. This has always annoyed me and largely how I ended losing respect for him as a man. I always saw how he allowed his mother and sister to take advantage of him. I actually stopped liking the mother and sister because of how they treated him. Whenever he decides to stand up for himself, they tell him that I must be in his ear and I'm trying to destroy his family relationship. I never encouraged him to disrespect his mother or sister, but I have told him to stop letting them take advantage of him. The mom feels if he doesn't conform to what she wants him to do, then he is disrespecting her. Honestly, one of the reasons I went to college out of state was to get away from his family—they were stressing me out and trying to break us up for years. He and I have been through alot and had a really close relationship. But when he started talking to this new girl, things changed. He started to feel himself and play mind games and tried to make me feel bad. After I exposed him to the new girl, showing her proof that he was playing her, he threatened to get a restraining order against me and tried to depict me as a crazy ex girlfriend who wouldn't leave him alone (he was calling me!). He cursed me out and said some very hurtful things to me. I recorded him saying he was using her and sent this recording to her. So yeah, he went HAM on me to give her the satisfaction, because he knew me and him were officially done and he didn't want to be alone (he admitted he's afraid to be alone).

I'm not mad about the breakup, but I am devastated as to how it ended. He only knew this girl for 4 months and she mistreated him horribly (disrespecting him and rubbing their relationship in my face) One minute he'll say how great she is. Then the next minute he explains how difficult, crazy and violent she is. And how she stresses him out. I don't understand how he could betray me for a chick he barely knows and we have a more solid history. For 2 months, he kept going back between the both of us and I got tired because he kept saying he was done with her but I found out they were still messing around. Hence, why I ended up exposing him to her and then cut him loose for good, which I did. I haven't talked to him in about 5 months and my heart is healing, but I still don't understand why he would risk losing me for a chick like her when I have been nothing but loyal and faithful to him, never took advantage of him and tried to help him grow. Even his mom admitted that I was a good woman, despite our differences. I will never understand this. But I'm grateful that i didn't have a baby with him nor did I lose sight of my aspirations and life goals due to my relationship drama. I'm still focused and about to start medical school soon. He still contacts me but I ignore him. My question is:

WHY DO YOU THINK HE BETRAYED ME SO DEEPLY, DESPITE ME ALWAYS BEING THERE FOR HIM?"

Avoid men who lack ambition and have a poor work history. A good indication of a man who is not self-motivated is one who is content working the exact same job since high school ten years later with no significant change in job title or pay. Clearly, the man in this letter also falls into the mama's boy category as well, but I'd like to talk about his lack of ambition. Believe it or not, I have counseled many women with similar stories. There are so many women with drive, ambition and determination in relationships with men whom they are trying to motivate. The writer is already becoming annoyed with the fact that her boyfriend does not share her passion, goals and success. If you are in a relationship with a man like this, your frustration will only deepen should you marry him. Allow a man to find himself before he finds you. If you know you want a traditional relationship where the man is the primary breadwinner and takes the lead role, you should not settle for a passive man who is not self motivated. You were designed to be the helper. The Bible calls this role the "help meet." It is not your responsibility to pick up where a man's mother left off. You are not helping him; you are enabling him if you continue to make decisions for him and not allow him to express his natural and primal urge to protect and provide for you. This could also be problematic in the future should you have children with a man who lacks ambition. Will he inspire your children to go after their dreams or will he dismiss their dreams as impossible, thereby encouraging them to embrace mediocrity? Either a man wants more for himself and his life or he does not. This case in particular is especially sad because I believe the boyfriend's mother has severely damaged her son's self-esteem. She has her own issues because her husband left her for another woman, so she is feeding into his insecurities by telling him things like, "She'll leave you for a man in college or medical school," and "If she really loved you she would have went to a local college." A man (or woman for that matter) with deeply ingrained self-esteem issues or an inferiority complex will need constant reassurance that he or she is enough.

Relationships with men like this are extremely exhausting. When determining if the man pursuing you has potential, you must evaluate him on who he currently is and not what you want him to be. Never date a man's potential; date who he is at the current moment. A man could have all the potential in the world, but if he never makes the conscious decision to tap into it, what good does it do him or the woman in his life? Sometimes as women we want "fixer uppers." A fixer upper is a man we feel we can mold and make into our ideal man. All he needs is a little push. Why do we feel the need to fix a broken man? Because it makes us feel all warm and fuzzy inside, that's why. We want to swoop in with our cape on and save the day. If you have ever flown anywhere you have heard the standard flight attendants' safety speech. They always say in the event of a crash you must put the oxygen mask on yourself first. Then, and only then, should you attempt to help others. As much as you want to motivate the man you love to reach his highest potential, resist the urge to put the oxygen mask on him first. You have to save yourself and he has to save himself. A man has to want to change on his own. We are nurturers by nature, so the desire to want to help someone in need is instinctual for us as women. The writer knew she wanted a man with more drive and ambition, and she's been with her boyfriend for over seven years, hoping that her ambition would rub off on him. According to life coach and author of the book "The Breaking Point: A Full Circle Journey" Michelle Hannah, you need a man who says, "Yes we can!" as opposed to "Why bother?" Lack of ambition should be one of your deal breakers because an incompatibility in this area significantly affects both of your views of your future. If he is comfortable in his minimum wage job and does not want more out of life, he may be content with renting an apartment and never becoming a homeowner or going on nice vacations, etc. If you, on the other hand, have dreams of working for a Fortune 500 company, earning a six figure salary and buying your first home by twenty-five, your lifestyles are not in sync. It is more likely he will pull you down to his level instead of you pulling him up to yours. If you learn nothing from this book, realize you cannot change a man. A man's love for you can inspire him to change, but it is still he who ultimately makes the decision himself to change. Your mate is a direct reflection of how you feel about yourself. The boyfriend in this letter did not end up with the other woman because she was smarter, prettier or more ambitious, but because she is what he felt he deserved. Always remember you attract what you feel you deserve. As commonsensical as it sounds, every relationship you enter into is not supposed to work because every man you date is not the one for you. Don't attempt to force a square peg into a round hole. If he is not what you want him to be the solution is simple, date another guy. The best way to avoid finding yourself in a similar situation is to pay close attention to a man's past and analyze how comfortable he is in his current situation. Is he too comfortable with mediocrity or is he determined to do something about it? Is a man of talk or action?

Next up, is the control freak. You have always been attracted to strong men who know what they want. So, when he is a bit aggressive initially you think it is sexy. He may tell you he prefers your hair up or you are with him now so you don't need to dress this way or that way. He wants to pick your friends. He liked your family and friends at first, but over time, he has discouraged you from being around them. He wants to be the only one in your life. He comes and goes as he pleases, but he gives you a hard time when you want to go out with your girlfriends. He has forbade you to have male friends because he does not trust them. Before you know it, it has been weeks or even months since you've spoken to people who you've talked to for years. He has isolated you to the point where you feel like he is all you have. You barely recognize yourself anymore because you have changed so much since being with him. You do not have to give up your identity and sense of self to be in a relationship. And any man who wants you to does not love you for who you are. Be leery of men who do not want you to speak to your own family and friends. Relationships that feel suffocating are not healthy. Men who want to move you away from the people who love you may not have your best interest in mind. If you feel like he is too aggressive and too controlling, leave the relationship. This type of man may become physically aggressive too. They want you to feel like they are all you have so you feel you have no one to turn to when the abuse begins. One of the best pieces of dating advice my father ever gave me is you never really know a man until you have seen him angry. When a man is angry, observe his behavior. Does he yell, punch the wall, scream at you, intimidate you, hit you or threaten to hit you? Does he leave you somewhere with no regard for your safety? Control freaks are overly critical and they are constantly trying to change you. When you met him, he liked the way you dressed, wore your make up or did your hair; now, he is trying to change things about you that seemed fine in the beginning. He discourages your relationships with everyone but him (i.e. your friends and family members). Some men attempt to get you as far away from your support system as possible so you are easier to control. Avoid men who are overly jealous. He is threatened by almost any and every man in your life. Whether he feels the waiter was paying you a bit too much attention while taking your order or he absolutely must know where you are at all times, be especially cautious. There's nothing wrong with a man showing his genuine concern but there is something wrong when you feel like he is trying to control every aspect of your life. Do not ignore these types of warning signs. This type of behavior is very dangerous and it can and most likely will escalate.

Next, there is the disappearing guy. You seem to get along great. When you are together, he acts as if he can't get enough of you. He is affectionate and attentive to your wants and needs. You had an amazing date on Saturday night, then...crickets. You can tell so much about a man by his level of consistency. He has not called, texted or even sent you an annoying "poke" on Facebook since that night. It's been days since you have seen or heard from him. Then, he returns out of nowhere as if nothing happened. You notice this is a cycle for him. Why does he just go missing? Where does he go? Men who disappear inexplicably are most often players. You may be his Saturday night girl, but there may be a Friday and Sunday night girl you know nothing about. He could be maintaining an actual relationship with someone else. If a man is genuinely interested in you and only you, he would not just disappear…unless, his feelings for you scare him. Perhaps he may genuinely be thinking you are the one and he is not ready for that level of commitment. He still wants his independence and fears he will lose his sense of autonomy if he enters a serious relationship with you (or anyone else for that matter). Make it clear to him that you are not into playing games and his constant disappearance and reemergence into your life make you doubt his sincerity. Let him know all you two will ever be is friends until he can be consistent. Say something like, "I'm not the type of girl who is easily moved by words. I'm more of an action type of girl. Don't just tell me you want to be in my life, show me." Allow him to make the next move and ensure that when he does he is not supplying you with vague answers. Another reason men disappear is they believe you may be too emotional and incapable of taking his constructive criticism, no matter how delicately it was delivered. He may have felt pressured into making more of commitment than he knew he was truly ready for. Or, you are simply not what he is looking for and he doesn't want you to attempt and conform yourself into being who you think he wants you to be.

Then, there is the mystery man. His stories never add up. One minute he says he never called you back last night because he accidentally left his phone in the back of a cab. However, when you ask him about it later, he says his phone actually died. He tells you he has to work late, yet comes home smelling freshly showered and smelling like cologne. He says he has been putting in a lot of overtime, but he does not have any extra money to show for it. Do not ignore the red flags and warning signs. A man's words must match his actions or the words are meaningless. Oftentimes, men who are inconsistent are cheating and trying to juggle two or more relationships. Watch out for a man who has passwords on all of his devices and takes his phone everywhere (he may even sleep with it under his pillow); he's always vague when you ask questions; he lies about everything, and he's flakey when it comes to making plans; and he's always on his phone). Do not make excuses for him or fill in the blanks yourself. When we're interested in a man we tend to give him a pass or two. Eventually, those passes catch up to us and we wonder why we allowed such behavior to go without consequences for so long. These passes turn into regret. When a man is interested in you, nothing and no one can keep him away. Likewise, if he is not interested, nothing you do or say will convince him to stay.

Next, there is the ladies man. He is irresistibly charming and has lots of female friends. In fact, you may have once been one of them yourself. Initially, you are flattered to receive so much attention from him. He loves the ladies, and the ladies love him. He assures you nothing is going on between them, but he is far too friendly with them for your liking. How exactly do you know if he is a ladies' man? The signs are all there. His phone is constantly ringing or vibrating with phone calls and text messages from his female "friends." You watch him smile or blush as he reads a text message, but he quickly dismisses it saying, "Oh, that's just one of my friends or home girls." It may seem like a huge ego boost at first that somebody like him would be interested in somebody like you, but you have a lot of work to do if you want to keep his attention. A ladies' man loves the attention he receives from other women. Whether he is interested in pursuing them or not, he is flattered that so many women enjoy his company. He loves the "I still got it" feeling he gets when he flirts with women who seem receptive to his charm. Being with a man like this can ultimately make you feel inadequate because no matter how much attention you shower upon him he still wants more than you alone can give.

Let's talk about the rolling stone next. At first meeting, he comes across as incredibly charming, handsome and attentive.

He later reveals to you that he has children. This may or may not be an issue for you. You may even have children yourself and the idea of a blended family is one you would gladly welcome. However, he lets you know he has children by a few different women. If this is the case, your antenna should immediately go up. Am I saying he is a bad guy? No, not necessarily, but a man who is irresponsible enough to continue having children with these women and then leave them to raise his child alone may not be relationship material. Who is to say he would not do the same to you? Do not let him convince you you're different and *you* are special to him. It is safe to say his exes may have gotten the same treatment at one time as well.

The jokester is next. He says he finds you attractive, but he rarely compliments you. He does, however, bring other attractive women to your attention. He insults you, but says he was just joking. He knows what your insecurities are and he exploits them. For example, he knows you are self-conscious about your hair, skin or weight, but he insists on making insensitive comments about those things. He has no problem laughing at your expense. In fact, you get the feeling he enjoys making you feel small and insignificant. When you tell him his comments bother you, he tries to make you feel like you're just being too sensitive and unable to take a joke. This is his attempt to break down your self-esteem. His goal is to make you feel like you are lucky to be with him and no one else wants you but him. Establish and maintain boundaries early on in the relationship. Be clear with him which topics are completely off limits and don't allow him to ignore your feelings. Speak up for yourself! If he ignores your requests, let him go. The man for you should not break you down – he should build you up.

Let's talk about the down-on-his-luck guy. Don't get me wrong, we all have difficult times here and there, but this guy just can't seem to get a break. He may have had some legal trouble in the past or lost his job but, for whatever reason, he has not been able to bounce back. He acts as if he is owed something. It does not take him long to start asking if you do not mind paying for a few things. Maybe his cell phone is about to be cut off or he is a little short on his rent. Perhaps he is having issues with his roommate or tired of living at home with his parents. He may ask to stay with you until he can "get back on his feet." Weeks turn into months and you don't see him making much of an effort to find a job. Some men seek to attach themselves to a well-established, independent or self-sufficient woman so she can take care of him. It is not your responsibility to take care of your boyfriend. Regardless of how much potential you think he has, if he is not actually utilizing that potential to better himself and his situation, you should end your relationship. Never let a man get too comfortable taking from you. Most decent men would feel uncomfortable and like less of a man to have their woman take care of them. If he does not seem bothered by this arrangement, be careful. Every leech needs a host. Do not allow him to bleed you dry.

We can't forget about the freeloader. There are times when a hard working man falls down on his luck. He may have been laid off or fired. Most hard-working men who enjoy providing for a woman are beside themselves and feel like less of a man when they cannot provide for the woman in their life because they have an instinctual need and desire to provide. Then, there is the freeloader. He can never hold down a job. He has had seven jobs in the last six years. He always has some excuse as to why this job or that job did not work out. He is very comfortable with you paying for things and treating him. In return, he is overly affectionate and loving. He may start out being extremely helpful around the house with chores, but that does not last long. You begin to notice he is not going on interviews, checking the classifieds or filling out applications, and he could not be bothered in the least. He is on the couch playing video games when you leave for work in the morning and he is still there when you return later that evening. The Bible says in 2 Thessalonians 3:10 "...if a man does not work he does not eat" (NIV). Be especially cautious of men who are too comfortable taking money from you, asking you for money or borrowing money you know they have no intention of paying back. Some men pursue well-established career driven women because they themselves do not want to earn their own living. A man does not necessarily have to make more money than you do, but he should at least be capable of taking care of himself financially.

Let's not forget the macho man. Of course, you want a man's man. He is a man who is dominant and in control, however, he is always right and you are not always wrong. You know the type. He could be exposed as dead wrong, but he would never admit it. To him it is a sign of weakness to acknowledge his flaws and shortcomings. The key to a successful relationship is compromise. You may not win every battle, so when it comes to compromising in a relationship make sure you are not always the one apologizing, bending or trying to make peace. For this relationship to last you must both be equally committed to seeing things from your partner's point of view.

Watch out for the cuddler. Let's be clear, if he was not sexually attracted to you he would never have asked you out. If the only door he rushes to open for you is the bedroom door he is most assuredly bad news. Beware of men who are in a rush to break the touch barrier. He wants a hug or even a kiss when you first meet him and every time after that you realize that he gets more and more touchy. He also likes to make sexual jokes or innuendos. It is almost as if he is unable to focus on anything else. He may say that you are not affectionate enough. He is always asking for more intimacy and constantly wants to know when he can come over. He suggests he cook for you at his place or "Netflix and chill." Be careful. Just chill can turn into to chill-dren! Once he gets you on his turf he will lay on the charm. A man being attracted to you is not the problem; a man who is only concerned with being intimate with you is. If he seems like he has a one-track mind it is probably because he does. Insist he take you on a real date and make it clear to him you are a woman of standards. This is not to say casual nights at home are a no-no. Be sure he is putting in the effort to get to know you and show you a good time. Let him know you are not the type of woman who comes over to his place in the middle of the night or gives affection to men you are not in a committed relationship with. Not sure how to say this without scaring him off? Try this, "I think you're an amazing guy and I can tell you're attracted to me. But, I'm not going to be pressured into doing anything I don't want to do. I am not interested in a strictly physical relationship with you or anyone else. I want something real." If he says he is okay with that yet insists on pressuring you, he has made his intentions clear. If he sticks around and changes his behavior, it is likely because he was impressed to see you had standards you are willing to stick to. You may have piqued his interest and now he is intrigued. This could be considered a bold move, but it is worth the risk. It proves to him your worth and self-respect mean more to you than a chance of being his girlfriend. Here are a few "he is only interested in sex" warning signs:

-He texts you almost exclusively (and when he does it is late at night).

-He tells you he's not ready for a relationship upfront, yet he is actively pursuing you.

-He has many attractive female friends, but he does not want to introduce you to them.

-He is reluctant to integrate you in any way into his life (i.e. meeting his family and friends).

-He forgets things you've told him.

-He is far too touchy feely.

-He is constantly commenting on your looks and/or your body.

-He often disappears without a valid explanation.

-Has never had a serious relationship for any reasonable amount of time.

-Your time together is primarily spontaneous; he does not take you on many planned dates.

-He insists on going Dutch. Beware of men who do not want to spend any money at all on you.

-He is always trying to get you alone.

-He only wants to talk about sex!

What about the guy at church? You've been praying to find your Mr. Right and the man God has for you, and suddenly you meet someone and think this must be him. He says and does all the right things. He prays with you and goes to church regularly. However, he admits he is struggling with being abstinent. Besides him going to church with you, he is a lot like the other guys that you've met. He may not be as direct about his interest in wanting to be intimate with you, but you are sure if you agreed he would not hesitate. Not all men you meet at church have ulterior motives, but some do. Some men attend church merely for the purpose of preying on vulnerable women. Do not forget what I told you earlier. You would be amazed at the lengths a man would go through just to be with you. Do not put yourself in compromising positions. Beware of men who are always trying to get you in one on one situations. Make sure the dates are out in the open. Do not engage in sexual conversations with him. If he insists on taking it to a sexual level then his motives are crystal clear. Make sure he is not only talking the talk, but also walking the walk. You should not be the only one feeling convicted if you are engaging in inappropriate behavior. If you feel like you are the only one concerned with doing what is right in the eyes of God, he is not the one. God would never send you someone who would confuse you or encourage you to violate God's law. Pray and ask God to make his intentions clear. Consider getting a Christian accountability partner to help you maintain your purity if you are abstinent. Establish real guidelines with the Christian guy you are dating. For example, holding hands and kisses on the cheek are fine, but no French kissing, no laying down together and no late night dates. This is why the spirit of discernment is so important. The Bible says "My sheep listen to my voice" (John 10:27 NIV). The more you are actively talking with God and getting His feedback on potential suitors, the easier it is to hear Him say whether he is the one or not. Prayer is a single girl's secret weapon.

Last but certainly not least, the unavailable man. Just because a man pursues you does not mean he is unattached. Unavailable men are currently involved with another woman. For some reason they are unfulfilled in their current relationship, so they pursue other women. He may approach you and begin flirting and trying to get to know you, but he doesn't reveal he is in a relationship. Unfortunately, some women make the assumption that if he were involved with someone he would never have approached them so they never ask and, of course, he never confesses. Like any other new courtship he pursues you and eventually you find out he has someone else. He then tells you he is unhappy in his current relationship but, by then, you are already emotionally invested and it is difficult for you to just end the relationship. You are put in a position you never expected to be in. You would never intentionally go after someone else's man, but you did not know. He promises to end the relationship, but time goes on and on and he never does. Check out this letter I received from a woman who was dating an unavailable man:

"Hello, I've been watching your videos lately and you have inspired and motivated me to become a stronger independent women. I've gotten involved in a pretty messed up situation lately. I met a man online who I have gotten into a relationship with. Around a month after getting to know him we started dating. Anyways about 4 months in the relationship I always had a feeling something was not right because 2 months in he told me he had just gotten out of a 9 year relationship with his ex and was still friends with benefits with her and that he has stopped being intimate with her. After about 2 weeks into knowing me I found out that they were still friends and hanging out. This bothered me during the whole entire time of our relationship and I have made it known to him. Anyways one day I stumbled across a photo that his ex posted. It was a gift from him and the date was during the time we started dating. I confronted him about it and he gave me lies at the time which I know now, because a few days later he broke down and confessed to me the complete truth that he was still in a relationship with her and that they lived together. I was shocked, but I kinda knew something was wrong. He told me that he wasn't intimate with her during our whole entire relationship and that he would go to bed after she was asleep and lay next to her with his back facing her & that they didn't even kiss or anything, which is hard to believe because he's a grown man, but his sex drive isn't very high so it is possible that could be true & he has only been with her besides me, so he doesn't have much experience in dating. Anyways I chose to stay, because he told me the truth and he did leave her 3 days after and moved out, like he said. It's been around 3 months since and we're still together but we still are having problems about this situation, a couple weeks ago I asked him to delete photos of her off his fb & he made a big deal about it, he eventually deleted them when I gave him an ultimatum that I was done with him if he didn't. We've gotten closer over the few months and I've learned to forgive him and not try to dangle his sin over his head. He admits that what he has done was wrong & out of character for him. He told me the reason he did it was because he was afraid of losing me and wishes he had left his relationship with her before he met me. He told me he has stopped loving her for a year and basically just stayed because it was comfortable, and that it's his fault and not mine that's why he's leaving her & he doesn't want me to think that he's leaving her for me. Anyways nearly 7 months now he's been wanting to have some time to himself to get his shit together, he says he's not ready to be anyone's bf right now but when he is he wants to be mine. He told me he still feels guilty for hurting her and he hasn't properly had closure with his ex. He also feels guilty when he see's me because he remembers how badly he's hurt me and that he's sorry for keeping me a secret, he plans to get his shit together, clean up his mess, explains to his friends & family about me, and find his own place in 2 months. Currently we're on a break now and I have agreed to this, but technically still together but with just no contact. Anyway I wanted your opinion on this I try to understand his situation because he's going through a big change right now in his life. Also that it must be hard for him because even tho he doesn't love her anymore they've been together for 10 years and that's 10 years of memories and he did leave in a rush, I feel bad for her too, but I also feel sorry for myself as well. I know he's a good guy and this is the only messed up thing he has ever done. I just want to be sure I'm not wasting anymore time with this man, because it is aldr right now, we have sent each other letters and gifts, but we plan to get together soon. He wants to have a fresh start with me after his 2 months. So should I give him his time & if it doesn't work out just cut him loose? Or should I save myself the time and just end it now? I always call him out on his lies but he tells me that he's really just needs time and that he does love me and wants to be with me & that he's just not ready yet, he's very confusing. In the beginning he wanted time apart but he kept delaying it until I insisted him to start it now, because I was tired of waiting for him to fully commit to us. He has introduced me to his dad and a couple friends but none of them really know who I am other than a "friend". I just wanted to know if you think it would be worth pursuing and giving a shot or what he says might just be a bunch of talk to string me along. We talk about the future a lot like marriage, living together, kids, our dreams, goals & even personal family stuff. So this makes me believe that I could actually have a real future with this guy. Sorry that this story is all over the place & Thank you for taking the time out of your day, God bless xo"

Don't be fooled by his elaborate excuses and logical explanations as to why he is still where he claims he no longer wants to be. When a new guy approaches you be sure to ask him if he is in a relationship. If he gives you an answer like, "It's complicated," or "Yes, but not for long," or "Something like that," keep moving. He is not a victim, but a willing participant in his own life. He created this situation for himself, and he does not deserve your sympathy or your pity. Make it clear to him you are a woman of high value and moral character and you would never willingly put yourself in a situation that is not an accurate depiction who you really are. You are no man's second choice. Stand your ground. Never allow yourself to be the third member in an already established relationship. Whether you believe in Karma or the law of sowing and reaping, you cannot plant negative seeds and not expect negative fruit. Men like this want to have their cake and eat it too. He is married, engaged or has a girlfriend but, for some reason, he has not ended the relationship. He tells you some sob story about he does not want to hurt her because he loved her once, but the love is gone, or he is only with her because of his child, or without her he has no place to stay. He pursues you relentlessly, doing and saying all the right things. Over time, you begin to let your guard down and start believing his lies. You begin settling for Christmas Eve or the day after Thanksgiving. He will never leave the other woman because he does not have to. Entertaining a man while he is admittedly still in a relationship with another woman says more about you than it does about him. Yes, of course he is a cheater, but you demonstrate a lack of standards and moral character by allowing this already attached man to attach himself to you. As we discussed earlier, don't let a man make a mistress or "other woman" out of you. Respect yourself enough to say, "I deserve a monogamous relationship with a man who values me and knows I'm worth more than sharing him with another woman."

Regardless of what you tell yourself, being the other woman confirms a lack of self-esteem. Don't you believe a man can love you and only you? If you struggle with low self-esteem, you must address that issue prior to pursuing a romantic relationship. Your relationship with yourself is the most important one you have. According to the book, "Conversations with God: An Uncommon Dialogue" by Neale Donald Walsch, the words I AM are two of the most powerful words in the English language. Whatever precedes the words *I am* is the ultimate declarative statement. Declare over yourself: "I am worthy of love," "I am fearfully and wonderfully made and the man for me will already know that," "I am worth more than a one night stand or being someone's mistress," and "I am enough!" Repeat these positive declarations daily if necessary. The more you say them the more you begin to believe them. When you are attempting to change your life or your behavior, you have to start small or you may become overwhelmed with the enormity of your ultimate goal. Make a conscious effort to take one small step towards changing this behavior every day. Progress may be gradual, but it is *still* progress. The first step in changing your life is to first change your mind. You attract what you believe you deserve. Convince yourself that you deserve better and better will be attracted to you.

CHAPTER TEN

Relationship Ready

By now you should have a pretty good idea about how and why men behave the way they do in relationships. You know the worst possible times to enter into a relationship with him, if he is playing you, the types of men to avoid and a lot more. You might be thinking, "Why should I even bother?" Not all men are like the ones described in this book. The problem is we often get involved with men who are simply not ready for a relationship. We tend to fall too hard and too fast for men who are only interested in keeping things casual or just a fling. We end up overinvesting in men who do not know our worth or who are not worth our time. I cannot tell you how many letters

I have received from women over the years with similar issues. I received a letter from a woman who said she was praying for a man then met one and wrongly assumed he was the one. Men who are interested in you or genuinely interested in seeing where things go with you are upfront about it. You should not have to decode his clues and signals. Knowing if a man is relationship ready will save you tremendous time, energy and potential heartbreak. In this chapter, let's talk about signs a relationship ready man would exhibit. Here are a few:

-He finds any and every excuse to be around you.

-He does not pressure you into being intimate.

-He is financially stable and where he wants to be in his career.

-He is attentive to your needs.

-He does not disappear without a reasonable explanation.

-He considers your opinion when making major plans.

-He is not afraid to be affectionate with you in public.

-He wants to learn more about you on a personal level.

-He opens up to you about his feelings.

-He is an open book.

-He keeps no secrets and will tell you anything you want to know.

-He has begun to integrate you into his daily life.

-He wants you to meet the people closest to him, like his parents and his best friend.

-He notices other attractive women, but you are always his main focus.

-You can tell he is attracted to you, but you can also tell he restrains himself to demonstrate how much he respects you.

-He makes future plans with you.

-What bothers you bothers him.

Let go of the idea that all of the good men are either married, gay or in jail. That is simply untrue. There are amazing, intelligent, God fearing, unattached men out there who want to find love just as badly as you do. In a research survey commissioned by Match.com called "Everything You Think You Know About Singles is Wrong: We Separate Fact from Fiction with the First Comprehensive Study of Singles in America" released on February 4, 2011, quite a few myths about men were dispelled. Renowned biological anthropologist Dr. Helen Fisher and social historian Stephanie Coontz conducted a study questioning over 5,000 men and women. The results are astounding:

"Single guys, who have long gotten a bum rap for being commitment-phobes and romantically blasé, are evidently misunderstood. The survey makes it clear: don't buy into these myths. Men fall in love faster, are more eager to have children for the first time (24% vs. 15%), and when it comes to love, feel just as intensely as women do. The most surprising fact about men may be this: "More men than women would marry a partner they weren't sexually attracted to," "Men are just as inclined to want to get married as women. In fact, 33% of men and 33% of women said they want to get married. And among singles without children under 18, more men (24%) than women (15%) say they want to have children."

These findings totally debunked just about every myth we have been told about men. As I mentioned in the very beginning of the book, it is not a matter of if a man wants to be in a committed relationship, it is a matter of when. He must be relationship ready for a relationship with him to work. I was speaking to a young man recently who wanted to be married and have children. His frustration with the fact that his search has not yet resulted in a meaningful relationship or lifelong commitment was evident. Hearing a man utter the same words I have heard women say to me for years was truly refreshing. He said, "I just want something real." Men want the same thing women want, but sometimes we just want those things at different times. It is entirely possible to meet the right man at the wrong time. This is not a matter of age but of relationship maturity. There are men well into their forties and fifties who are still playing the field, and there are also men who are in their early twenties who are looking to settle down and be in a committed monogamous relationship.

Let go of the past. Unfortunately, we don't always get the closure we need from our past relationships, so the burden falls upon us to find an end to those situations so we can be free and open to finding love with someone else. I often hear of women who have been in an on and off relationship with the same man for five, ten or even twenty years. They carry on these relationships because there was never real closure and because the door was never shut and locked; it was easy for an ex to regain entry into their lives. We leave the door to our past open for several reasons. We think, "I've invested far too much time to start all over with someone else," "Being with him is better than being alone," "At least he wants me," or "One day he will realize I'm perfect for him and he'll change." This emotional yo-yo relationship will keep you in a constant state of confusion and hinder you from finding and exploring love with someone who has no doubts about what you mean to him. After all these years your ex is still not convinced you are the one or he would have committed to you and not risk you finding love with another man when he was not around. If he wanted to be with you, he would have been. Don't allow him and his empty promises to waste one more second of your time. There's a quote that reads, "Never ask a shirtless man for the shirt off his back." If an ex cannot offer you what you know you deserve, reject that offer and move on. Stop allowing him to regain access to your life after you've made what you want clear and he has made it clear that he is unable or unwilling to give that to you.

Men are not the only ones who have to be relationship ready for it to work. Let's discuss ways to make you relationship ready. Be open minded. There is nothing wrong with having a type or preferences, but it is also important to consider the complete package. A friend of mine was thinking of asking a woman out. He was a bit gun shy so he engaged her in several conversations just to feel her out and see if he could possibly be her type. He is well educated, attractive and caring. She mentioned to him she was vegetarian. This was not an issue for him, but she then told him she was not interested in men who were not. She said it would be a real hassle trying to accommodate both of their food preferences so she would rather not date a man who ate differently than she did. I was amazed she would disqualify my friend so easily. There is a huge difference between a deal breaker and a flaw. The more he told me about their conversations the more I realized she was the one with the issue. She wanted to date the male version of herself. As cliché as it sounds, "nobody's perfect." You cannot expect perfection from him when you are flawed. You want a man who is six feet with a six pack making six figures, yet you know you have picked up quite a bit of weight since college and your bank account is constantly overdrawn. If you expect him to love you despite your shortcomings, he must be afforded the same courtesy. He may leave the toilet seat up, forget to put the cap back on the toothpaste or leave the kitchen a mess every time he cooks, but is he a good man and is he good to you? Some call it the 80/20 rule. Does he meet the majority of your needs? If he does you have to decide if it is more important to you to win the battle or win the war. He may be annoyed that you wear your headscarf to bed, can be a bit OCD about housework or love reality television shows. The right man can come to find these things endearing. Early on in my relationship with my husband, he would make fun of me all the time for my obsession with sunflower seeds and now he buys them for me by the case.

Be confident. They say the sexiest thing a woman could wear is confidence and that statement could not be truer. You do not have to be the prettiest, smartest or thinnest girl to get a man's attention. Truth is, you just have to be comfortable in your own skin and secure in who you are. Basically, you have to own it! Men have an innate ability to detect low self-esteem and a woman's insecurities from a mile away. They like to feel like being with you is almost like winning a prize. I always tell my husband (half jokingly), "Out of all the many men in the world I could have chosen I chose you." He usually blushes because he knows I am completely serious and partially because knows it is true. Sometimes without evening knowing it we show our insecurities to men. For example, constantly pointing out attractive women to him and asking, "Do you think she is pretty?"highlights an insecurity. Don't downplay yourself just to make him feel better. If he pays you a compliment and tells you that you look beautiful for your date, don't say something like, "Me? I look okay, but YOU look like you could be in GQ magazine or something." Comments like this will instantly lessen his level of attraction for you. Learn how to take a compliment. Just say "Thank you" and not "Thank you but…" Accept the kind words and realize they are coming from a genuine place. The person saying them honestly means what they are saying. I'll let you in on a little secret. Confidence is an inside job. It is a belief in yourself that manifests itself in the way you walk, talk, carry yourself, and even accept compliments. No one is going to think you are beautiful, intelligent and sexy if you do not think so yourself. Try saying these things to yourself in the mirror. The more you say amazing things about yourself the more you begin to believe them.

Get rid of your defense mechanisms and the lies you have been telling yourself. You must change the narrative to the story you have been telling yourself for years. We believe these untruths and adopt them as fact. Here are a few examples of the lies that we tell ourselves as protection from the threat of rejection:"Men are intimidated by my success," "I don't need a man," "I'm single because I need to lose weight," "I'm single because I cannot compete with other women," "Men don't find me attractive," "No man will ever want to be with a virgin," "No man will want to be with someone who has a debilitating illness or chronic disease," "No man wants to raise another man's children," "Most men are players anyway," "All the good guys are already taken," "A man will not be interested in someone as quirky as I am," or "I'd be lucky to have any man." LIES! Every last one of those statements is a lie. You have to silence your inner critic. It's that little voice in your head that tries to convince you that you are even happier alone or you are unworthy of the type of love you know in your heart you deserve. This kind of thinking is counterproductive and does not serve you. Take a moment to be honest with yourself. What lies are you telling yourself? Those lies could be sabotaging your love life.

Resolve your unresolved issues. You must be both physically and emotionally ready to start a new relationship. It is unfair to the other person and yourself to pursue a relationship with someone new, knowing your heart belongs to someone else. Settling for your number two guy can bring catastrophic complications. Take this letter for instance:

"Hi BG,

I've been a huge fan of your channel and strawberry letters for quite some time, and need you to get me together on the mess

I've recently made of my life. I know your disdain for long letters so I'll try to keep this short.

I am 32 years old and have had a male best friend for the past 12 years. We dated briefly for a few months but he was a bit rough around the edges at the time when I was seeking a husband so I "friend-zoned" him. Shortly thereafter, I met a great guy who checked all of my boxes and was the opposite of my friend in every way: great career, master's degree, financially stable, homeowner, strong Christian beliefs, etc. but we never had the passion, connection or chemistry of what I experienced with my best friend. A few weeks before my wedding my friend came into town (he lives in another state) and we ended up having a hot and heavy make-out session. I knew at that moment that HE was "the one" but it was too late. Despite 4 years of dating and the recent episode with my best friend, I married the good guy (he wouldn't allow my friend to attend our wedding) and we've now been married for

5 years. My friend resents the fact that I am the one that got away, but we remained close.

Throughout the years my husband grew increasingly uncomfortable with our behavior (talking on the phone for hours, nicknames, sending pics, thousands of texts, etc.) and questioned several times if we were having an affair. Emotional perhaps, but not physical. He even gave us ultimatums but we just couldn't end our friendship. I fell in love with my friend, and he loved me too, but what could we do? I was now stuck in a marriage. The situation naturally soured the relationship with my husband and even when I tried to do the right thing and let my friend go, we were like magnets and always found ourselves drawn back to each other.

Three years into the marriage, I went to visit my friend for his birthday (without my husband's knowledge) and it was the first time we've seen each other since that hot night prior to me walking down the aisle. One thing led to another and we ended up having sex for the first (and only) time in our 12 year history. Shortly thereafter I discovered I was pregnant. I didn't regret the affair but was ashamed that we didn't use protection. My friend was excited to be a father yet scared because I was married with more to lose. Life finally presented me with a way out and I had to make a decision. Due to the stress of the situation and being unsure of who's child I was carrying (my husband and I tried for years to conceive) I decided to pass the pregnancy off as my husband's, distance myself from my best friend, and recommit to my marital vows of letting my husband be the only man in my life.

When the baby was born my best friend and I quickly realized that this was OUR baby (my husband and best friend look nothing alike). However, the pressure of the secret coupled with my friend's hurt and bitterness of watching my husband (through social media) raise his son finally tore us apart. The two men in my life have never met in person. Fast forward through a year consumed with incredible heartache, what-ifs, missed first milestones of our son and an ended friendship, I eventually reconnected with my friend. Unbeknownst to me, he recently relocated to my state due to a new job but no longer wants the responsibility of being a father. He felt like he was treated as a sperm donor, is now in a serious relationship, and doesn't want anything to do with me or our son. I was devastated.

After carrying such a weighted secret for so long, I confessed everything to my husband. Although he was furious, he's very private and doesn't want to pursue divorce or a paternity test. I'm not sure what to do. My husband can provide the better life for my son but I can't get over my best friend. It's hard to grit my teeth and go through the motions of an emotionally empty marriage when my son's face reminds me everyday of my one true love. I question if I should stay in my marriage or fight to work things out with my soul mate (especially now that we live in the same state). I've prayed about the situation but mentally can't let it go and am left wondering, did I make a mistake and miss my fate?"

If you are in a situation with someone you were once romantically involved with, it is best to break all ties. As demonstrated by this letter, the "friend zone" is where some women put men who are not exactly what they want (or want at the time) but have potential. You keep him around because he is safe. Unlike with other men, you have no fear he will reject you because he has already made his intentions clear. Rather than letting him go completely so he can be free to fully love someone who loves him just as he is, we selfishly keep him around for own benefit. Either pursue the relationship and see where it goes or let him go completely, but don't maintain the relationship under the guise of an innocent friendship when you know one or both of you has developed feelings for the other. As the writer stated, it is easy to wonder "what if," and you begin to question the love you have for your current mate. Unbeknownst to your new love interest he is in competition with your "friend" or your "ex." End all communication with any man who potentially poses a threat to your new relationship. Fantasy is often better than reality. We paint a vivid picture in our minds of how it could be with the ex or friend, but in reality it is the ultimate unknown. Who is to say things will be different with the ex this time? As they say, "An ex is an ex for a reason." Who is to say the man in the friend zone is as good of a boyfriend as he is a friend. Never sacrifice what is real for what is imagined.

A broken woman will attract a broken man or a man who enjoys fixing broken women. Both scenarios have bleak outcomes. Two broken individuals cannot maintain a healthy relationship. A man who wants a broken woman may grow tired of you when you become better because he has to address his need for wanting to fix what is broken.

Let go of past insecurities. Whether it stems from issues in our childhood, our relationship with our parents or even past relationships with men, we need to resolve these issues if we ever hope to have productive relationships with a significant other. Take this scenario for example: you were in a long term relationship with your ex-boyfriend, and you were madly in love with him. You talked about getting married, buying a house together and eventually starting a family. You even had names picked out for your future children. You later find out he had been cheating almost the entire relationship and you are understandably devastated. Expectedly, you develop trust issues. You meet a new guy who is amazing and definitely interested in being with you. You want to check his phone, you want him to give you the password to his social media accounts, and you give him a hard time every time he wants to go out with his friends. You have begun to project your past hurt and mistrust from your ex-boyfriend on to him. If you fail to acknowledge there is an issue, you will sabotage every relationship you are in. Whether your issue is being molested as a child, growing up without a father, being teased about your weight, being cheated on, etc., you have to speak to someone about these feelings to find ways to cope with them. There is no shame in going to counseling or speaking with a therapist or life coach. Therapy can help you heal so you are not broken and expecting your new man to help put you back together. You want a man who sees you as a partner and not a project. There are men who are incredibly patient and loving and they will hold your hand, be your shoulder to cry on and support you while you deal with your past, but if you can identify these issues on your own, why wait for someone else to save you? Put the life vest on and save yourself. Seeking help to resolve past hurt and pain is an investment in yourself and your own well-being.

Celebrate your femininity. You are sugar and spice and everything nice. Don't you just love being a girl? There is nothing wrong with showing your softer side and letting a man see a bit of your vulnerability. This is not just about wearing makeup, a beautiful dress and a pair of six inch heels, although there is absolutely nothing wrong with that. In fact, if that is what you are into, go for it! This is more about the emotional side of being a woman. Society makes us feel like showing our softer side is a sign of weakness. To overcompensate, we can sometimes come across far too aggressive, competitive, argumentative and sometimes even too masculine. To put it bluntly, if a man wanted to be surrounded by masculine energy, he would play basketball with his friends, grab a drink with a male coworker after work or watch the big game at a sports bar. When a man is with you, he wants to be surrounded by your feminine energy. We all have a bit of a masculine and a feminine side. As a woman, you may express the more masculine side at work when you are making a presentation in the boardroom or on the phone trying to land a big client, but when you are in your quiet time with your mate or a potential suitor, this is the time to express your feminine side. This is when you should relish the opportunity to be flirty, compassionate, playful, confident and sexy. It is all about balance. You don't have to prove to him how tough you are and he does not need you to.

Lastly, get a life, get a man. You may be thinking I have that backwards but, I promise you, I do not. Men are attracted to women who are enjoying life. Picture this, a man is attracted to two women in a bar. Woman A is sitting alone in a corner looking miserable. Her jaw is clenched, her arms are crossed and she looks like she would rather be anywhere but there. Then there is Woman B. She is smiling and laughing so hard her eyes are starting to water. She is dancing in her chair, snapping her fingers and moving her body to the rhythm of the music. Who do you think he would approach? Meeting a woman with a full life is like getting into an exclusive club – of course he wants to be part of that! So, how do you live a life that makes a man want to be a part of it? Simple. You start living your ideal life now. Get out more! I recently read a book called, "The Power of Now" by Eckhart Tolle. What a life changing book that was! In the book, Tolle talked about the importance of savoring and appreciating the present moment. So many of us live in the past or the future, but rarely do we live in the now. You convince yourself everything will be so much better when you're married. As a single woman, I am sure you have envisioned the amazing life you will share with the man of your dreams, but I want this book to encourage you to live that amazing life now. I once heard this story by Esther Hicks, co-writer of several books such as "The Law of Attraction." She said she was once in the Dallas International Airport on her way to another destination. She said the airport was absolutely beautiful. There was amazing food, places to shop, and stations where you could plug in your gadgets. Then she found out her flight had been delayed. She saw this as an amazing opportunity to explore the airport a bit more. While enjoying a massage she received word that her flight had now been cancelled. She thought briefly to herself, 'Now what?' but she continued on, optimistically. Even though things were not happening when and how she wanted them to happen, she would still enjoy the journey. She discovered that attached to the Dallas International Airport was a Grand Hyatt. Upon checking into the hotel, she thought it was one of the most beautiful hotels she had ever stayed in. Later, when reflecting on the events of the day she thought to herself, 'What an amazing journey on my way to an amazing journey.' I believe that is exactly how a woman should approach her single life. Look at it with a sense of optimism. Appreciate the journey on your way to the next journey. You are not waiting for Christmas to open your gifts – you are opening them now. You will not delay or postpone your happiness, but seek it out and savor every moment of it. Go on that ski trip, take that cooking class, go to that poetry reading and book that trip to Paris. Life does not begin when you meet the man of your dreams. It has already begun and it can be as amazing as you are willing to allow it to be. Love where you are, for this is only a season...and seasons change.

CONCLUSION

As I said in the introduction, the purpose of this book was to help you understand men. They say men are from Mars and women are from Venus but, truthfully, I don't believe we are all that different. Ultimately, we all want the same things. We want to be in a loving committed relationship with someone who will allow us to be ourselves, acknowledge our value, appreciate us and never exploit our vulnerabilities. This book was not an opportunity to bash men. I love men far too much to ever do that. This book was written to help you identify when a man is not being upfront, not ready or simply uninterested in a serious relationship. This knowledge is meant to help you to decipher, decode and even dismiss (if necessary) men with bad intentions or men who are not ready for the level of commitment you're ready for. This will save you precious time. I hope I have succeeded in making these distinctions as clear as possible. Thank you from the bottom of my heart for purchasing this book and reading it with both an open mind and an open heart. It is my sincere hope you will find the love you have always dreamed of and it will be even more fulfilling and even more mind blowing than you ever imagined.

SPECIAL THANKS

Huge thanks to my amazingly talented and patient editor Kim Elliott-White and my cover designer Clara Debnam of fortknoxMEDIA. It was an honor and privilege working with each of you on this project.